Write Your Name
in KANJI

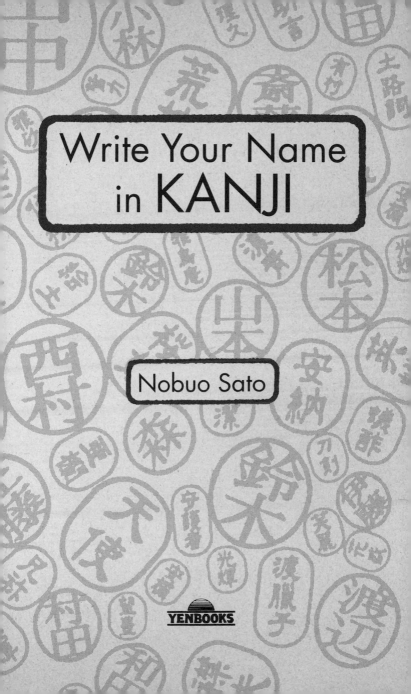

Write Your Name in KANJI

Nobuo Sato

YENBOOKS

YENBOOKS
2-6, Suido 1-chome, Bunkyo-ku, Tokyo 112, Japan

© 1996 by YENBOOKS

LCC Card No. 95-60908
ISBN 4-900737-35-6

First edition, 1996

Printed in Japan

Table of Contents

Preface

When going to a foreign land, whether for work or for play, it is common sense that the better able you are to adapt to local ways, the more successful your trip will be. One way in which the traveller might adapt to the ways of another country is by changing his or her name to fit local custom. For example, when in Rome, a wise American by the name of Charles may call himself Carlos; a smart English lady named Juliet might call herself Giulietta.

Japan, more than most countries, places an emphasis on harmoniously blending in with others.In fact, it has not one, but two proverbs similar to the Western one about doing in Rome as the Romans: *Go ni itte wa, go ni shitagae,* or "Obey the customs of the village you enter"; and *Deru kugi wa utareru,* or "The nail that sticks up will be hammered." This suggests, then, that the Westerner who manages to leap across the cultural chasm and adapt his or her name to the vernacular is taking the first step toward a happy and productive stay among the Japanese.

This book is intended to help you easily determine the most suitable way of rendering your name into Japanese. Even though an English name might not have an equivalent Japanese name, *Write Your Name in Kanji* will help you understand what goes into selecting a name, and will present a number of choices so that you can pick the most appropriate characters to represent your own name in Japanese. In doing so, this book may even help give you a better understanding of your own original, English name.

As you will see, you may consider several different Japanese equivalents for your name and select the one most appropriate to your tastes and character. If you are not satisfied with the meaning carried by your original English name, chances are that you can find a name approximating it phonetically but containing a fabulous meaning that your English name lacks. You may decide to use one of the "attention-getting transcriptions" to amuse your friends or deliver such an unforgettable first impression that new business associates will never forget you. If you stick to the original meaning of your English name, you may also find a corresponding one in fascinating kanji. If you prefer a simple phonetic transcription, you can simply elect to render your name in its katakana or hiragana equivalent.

Even if your name happens to be one of those that occurs rarely (or never) in English, with the result that there is no entry for it in this book, you needn't despair! You can render your name phonetically, making use of the *katakana, hiragana, or even kanji* provided in the charts provided for this purpose.

Once you've selected a name that appeals to you, you might even have it engraved into a *hanko* (a seal or stamp always required in lieu of a handwritten signature for official or business-related documents) and officially register it with your city hall. They, in turn, will issue a certificate legitimizing your seal, and the characters it bears, as legally valid and binding on any official document to which you affix it.

The author sincerely hopes that this book will help you and your friends to succeed in "doing in Japan as the Japanese do," and contribute to your building happy relationships with your Japanese friends.

For their valuable ideas the author wishes to thank Messrs. Yoshie Shimizu and Yoshio Ogasawara. The author especially wishes to thank the editor Mr. David Friedman for his professional advice and full cooperation.

Nobuo Sato,
Toride City, Ibaraki Prefecture, Japan

How To Use This Book

Understanding Japanese writing

Before getting started, we should note a few points about the Japanese language. First, there's the phonetic system: for the purpose of simplicity, this book uses the following letters to represent the following sounds:

a   as in "father"
e   as in "egg"
i   as in the "ee" sound in "feet"
o   as in "boat"
u   as in "prune"

On a somewhat longer note, we need to understand some basics about how Japanese writing works. There are three types of script in Japanese: kanji, hiragana, and katakana (the latter two are collectively referred to as *kana*). Kanji are ideographic characters, meaning that each of them represents not just a sound, but an object or idea. Used in China since the sixteenth century B.C., they arrived in Japan some two millenia later. Until then, Japan had had no system of writing at all.

Some simple examples of kanji are:
人   person   (pronounced *hito,* or *jin*)
火   fire (pronounced *hi,* or *ka*)
和   harmony (pronounced *wa*)

At first, Japanese used kanji only as phonetic symbols, with no regard for their actual meaning. As a result, a simple word like 体 *(karada)*, meaning "body," might, for example, have been written with characters such as 化羅打 (respectively: *ka,* "change," *ra,* "silk gauze," and *da,* "hit"), whose meanings bear no relevance at all to the intended meaning. Having to write so elaborately even to depict simple words proved wearying and, by the end of the first millenium, a phonetic "shorthand" script based on kanji, hiragana, appeared, followed shortly by katagana. The roles and forms of kanji and kana have changed throughout the centuries. In contemporary times, kanji are almost always used for their meanings exclusively (with rare exceptions, called *ateji,* still occuring here and there). Hiragana are primarily used for words whose kanji are excessively difficult and obscure, as endings for some kanji-based words, and for particles. Katakana are used mainly for foreign words and to emphasize native words, serving a role similar to that played by italics in English.

History of transcription

This book hardly represents the first attempt to render foreign words into kanji. Especially in the latter half of the nineteenth century, as Japan awakened from her long, isolated slumber and started to have contact with the outside world, the problem of how to write foreign words (such as country names) arose. At first, Japanese adhered to the old tradition of writing words with kanji chosen for their pronunciations, rather than their meanings. Some examples of transcriptions from that era include:

亜細亜	Asia	欧羅巴	Europe	亜米利加	America
加奈太	Canada	仏蘭西	France	伊太利亜	Italy
秘露	Peru	倫敦	London	伯林	Berlin

At the same time, there was a growing trend toward using katakana to represent foreign words, such as names and the techinical terms that started flooding into Japan when she opened herself to the West and its technology. Finally, in 1902, the Ministry of Education issued a list of standardized katakana renditions of Western personal and place names (for East Asian ones, the original kanji were simply retained). Since then, it has been regarded as proper to use katakana to represent non-Japanese words and names. Kanji still surfaces occasionally, though, especially as abbreviations for country names in newspaper headlines.

What's in a name?

English names are not just random and meaningless collections of sounds. Virtually all "conventional" names do, or at least did, have very clear meanings when they were first concocted. Many English names are rooted in old Hebrew words used in the Bible, terms from old West European languages, or words from ancient Greek and Latin. For instance, let's look at the following examples:

Adelaide (f) A compound of the Old German, "noble" and "type" (corresponds to the English suffix "-hood"). (EGW).

Edward (m) A compound of the Old English, "rich" and "guardian." (ECS)

Phyllis (f) From the Greek, "leafy." (EGW)

Sylvia (f) Latin feminine of Silvius, derivative of *silva,* "wood" (EGW).

In contemporary times, many Westerners no longer think much about the original meanings of names, being content simply to select names that appeal to them for sundry reasons unrelated to meaning. In East Asia, however, meaning is a very important part of picking a name. Since kanji are ideographic, one can tell at a glance what a person's name means. As a result, picking an appopriate meaning is central to selecting the right name.

Putting it all together

By this point, we've gotten a basic understanding of how the Japanese writing system works, and we've talked a little bit about what goes into picking names, both English and Japanese. Let's move on, then, and talk about what's really at the heart of this book. How do we go about transcribing English names into Japanese?

The key to successfully rendering an English name into Japanese script is deciding what we want to achieve. For instance, many people will want kanji that retain both the pronunciation and the original meaning of their names. Others may not care so much about meaning, so long as the pronunciation is retained. Different people will want different things out of their kanji. Along these lines, for each of the English names included in this book, up to six categories of transcriptions are provided.

Kana transcription: This is the standard method of writing English (and other non-Asian) names in Japanese script. While katakana is usually used for this purpose, some people prefer hiragana, thinking it more aesthetically pleasing. Kana transcription is the simplest method for writing English words in Japanese, and is especially useful for newcomers to Japan or new Japanese-language students.

Example: Linda, written in katakana, would be transcribed as リンダ (rinda).

Purely phonetic transcription: This method simply combines characters whose sounds approximate the English name being rendered into Japanese. It completely ignores the characters' meaning, considering only their pronunciation. Since meaning is irrelevant in this category of transcription, enterprising readers may wish to try producing especially pleasing kanji compounds by mixing and matching identically pronounced kanji. Even if you can't read kanji, you can still swap them around as long as they occupy similar positions in their compounds (for instance, you might swap the second kanji in one compound for the second kanji in another compound).

Example: Karen might appear as 歌連 or 華連. Or, you might swap the first kanji in the two compounds and make two new ways to write Karen: 歌連 and 華連.

Purely denotative transcription: This method is the opposite of the one previously described. Disregarding pronunciation, this way of transcription focuses solely on preserving the meaning of the original English name. To be able to do a denotative rendering, it is necessary to know the original meaning of the English name; those meanings appear in this book for that purpose.

Example: Edward (from the Old English for "rich guardian") could be transcribed thus: 富裕保護者 , meaning "rich guardian," and pronounced *fuyu hogosha.*

Phonetic and denotative transcription: This is the method that's got it all: sound, and meaning, too. As you might imagine, few (and occasionally no) appropriate choices are left by the narrow constraints imposed by using both sound and meaning as criteria for picking kanji.

Example: David (which originally means "darling") can be written 出 美奴 . The pronuciation becomes *debido,* while the meaning is "good-looking fellow," or, by association, "darling."

Phonetic and eulogistic transcription: These transcriptions retain the phonetic aspect of the English name, while using kanji that speak pleasantly of the person himself: they may depict images of wisdom, power, wealth, social standing, etc. While generally irrelevant to the original meaning of an English name, they may on the other hand convey provide a measure of elan that the original name lacks.

Example: Bruce (originally a Norman place name), can be written as 務 瑠守 , or "one who is in charge of keeping gems."

Attention-getting transcription: Attention-getting transcriptions are similar to the previously explained type of transcription in the way they work. The only difference is that rather than using characters with good meanings, they tend to be comical or even negative. They are calculated to attract people's attention and to make sharp impressions on business clients and partners and may therefore be especially suitable for foreign businessmen in Japan for whom it is critical to make an indelible first impression.

Example: Hillary (from the Latin for cheerful) can be written as 疲驪里
萋 , or "a tired sick mule in the village."

A final category of transcription appears, as well. Occasionally, I have added what I call "brainteasers." A brainteaser is phonetically faithful to the original English name, but offers a kind of puzzle that may pique people's interest and provoke them to ask you why it represents the original English name. The humor and creativity of the brainteaser's connection to the English name is sure to indelibly print your name into the memories of your friends and business associates.

A few final thoughts on transcription, and the kanji used in this book. As some readers may know, the Ministry of Education currently has a list of 1,945 characters (常用漢字, *joyo kanji,* or "common-use characters") "recommended" for use in government documents, education, publishing, etc. Ideally, according to the Ministry, no written communication should go out of the bounds represented by these kanji. Even so, people often eschew this rule as restrictive, people often go out of the boundaries anyway, using many kanji in their everyday lives that do not appear on the standard list.

The joyo kanji, in fact, represent a relatively small percentage of the entire number of existing kanji. In searching for appropriate kanji for Western names, therefore, the author has often found it necessary to break out of the 1,945-character boundary imposed by the joyo kanji list and search even among more difficult and obscure kanji to find characters that best fit certain names. This is not, in fact, unusual, as Japanese themselves often have names whose characters are outside the pale of joyo kanji and are unreadable even to other Japanese.

It is important that you keep this in mind, for even as your Japanized name will delight most of your friends, it will also disturb a few, who will claim that they have never seen the characters before and may even disparage it for its unconventionality. Yet, should this happen, it is they who are being blinded to their own cultural heritage by narrow-mindedness. Rendering names into kanji on the basis of pronunciation alone, and/or into obscure characters is, after all, an important part of Japanese orthographic culture, as we have seen.

Whichever transcriptions you end up liking the best, it is my hope that this book will succeed in conveying to you some of the beauty and pleasure of one of the world's oldest and most elegant writing systems. Serving as both words and pictures, kanji are not only a tool to enable written communication, but for the non-Asian, a window into some of the mystery and grandeur of an ancient and fabulous culture. It is the author's hope that with the aid of this book, non-Asians, too, can bring some of that special quality to their own names.

Kanji
for
First Names

Aaron
(m) Hebrew, "lofty mountain" (ECS)

Kana transcription: アーロン／あーろん

Purely phonetic transcription: 噫論　阿阿倫　亜阿崘
雅阿崙　堊亜崙　椏雅論　鴉亜崙　阿亜論
亜雅論 and also 阿倫　亜崙　雅崙　堊崙　鴉崙

Purely denotative transcription: 高峰 = a lofty ridge, *takamine*; 高山 = a lofty mountain, *takayama*; 高峻 = loftiness, *koshun*; 嵯峨 = loftiness, *saga*; 斗峻 = loftiness, *toshun*; 峭峻 = loftiness, *shoshun*.

Phonetic & denotative transcription: 雅亜崙 = an elegant Asian sacred mountain = hence a "lofty mountain".

Phonetic & eulogistic transcription: 雅亜論 = one who has an elegant Asian theory, hence an elegant Asian theorist; 雅論 = one who has an elegant theory = hence an elegant theorist.

Attention-getting transcription: 鴉雅論 = a crow which has an elegant theory; 唖蛙論 = a laughing frog's theory; 阿鴉乱 = a violent African crow; 蛙雅乱 = a frog's elegant uprising.

Brainteaser: 孤独 = to be alone, hence a lonely person. Note: "Aaron" (= alone) = 孤独 in Japanese. Hence it is read "Aaron."

Abbey
(f) Pet form of Abigail (LDGW); see Abigail

Kana transcription: アビー／あびー

Purely phonetic transcription: 雅鼻意　唖肥威
亜魅尉　阿眉医　雅備慰

Purely denotative transcription: See Abigail

Phonetic & denotative transcription: 婀毘慰 = a pretty woman who is helpful and consoling, hence "a lady's maid."

Phonetic & eulogistic transcription: 雅備医 = an elegant female doctor; 婀美衣 = a beauty in beautiful clothes; 婀魅威 = a beauty with charm and dignity; 唖美威 = a dignified smiling beauty.

Attention-getting transcription: 蛙備威 = a frog endowed with dignity; 鴉尾偉 = a crow having a great tail.

Abigail
(f) Hebrew, "a father's joy"; now synonymous with "a lady's maid" (HS)

嬪御

Kana transcription: アビゲール／あびげーる

Purely phonetic transcription: 阿日下江流
阿美夏絵留　雅美戯柄瑠　亜美霞衛琉
椏比芽慧劉 and also 婀備詣瑠　亜眉迎留　阿美夏留

Purely denotative transcription: 父乃歓喜 = a father's joy, *chichi-no-kanki*; 親父乃欣喜 = a father's joy, *oyaji-no-kin-ki* or 女官 = a lady's maid, *jokan*; 官女 = a lady's maid, *kanjo*; 嬪御 = a lady's maid, *hinjo*.

Phonetic & denotative transcription: 婀毘下営留 = a pretty helping woman of a low rank = hence a lady's maid.

Phonetic & eulogistic transcription: 雅備芸留 = an elegant person who is endowed with artistic talents; 婀美華漏 = an brilliant beauty; 阿魅迎留 = a charming African receptionist; 唖美詣留 = a smiling beauty worshiping at a shrine.

Attention-getting transcription: 蛙備牙柄留 = a frog with a tusk. 鴉尾下重留 = a crow having a heavy drooping tail.

Adam
(m) Hebrew, "man of red earth" (ECS)

仇務

Kana transcription: アダム／あだむ

Purely phonetic transcription: 亜打無　阿陀舞
雅舵務　堊妥武　亜驒夢　阿柁霧　椏堕矛
仇務　讐無　徒霧　敵眸

Purely denotative transcriptions: 赤土男 = man of red earth, *sekidonan* or *akatsuchiotoko*; 赤人 = red man, *akahito* or *akato*; 赤膚 = red skin, *akahada*.

Phonetic & eulogistic transcription: 亜打武 = an Asia-beating warrior; 阿蛇務 = an African snake charmer; 雅陀舞 = an elegant Buddha's dance; 仇武 = a revenging samurai.

Attention-getting transcription: 蛙唾霧 = a frog's saliva spray; 窪蛇無 = no snake in the hollow; 蛙打務 = a frog beater.

Brainteaser: 初代男 = the first man; 楽園住人 = a dweller in paradise.

Adrian
(m) Latin, name of a city in Northern Italy (LDWG)

Kana transcription: エイドリアン／えいどりあん

Purely phonetic transcription: 英度利案　叡土理安
栄鳥庵　営鶏鞍　映奴哩杏　永鳥安 or 亜土利案
阿土理安　雅鳥庵　亜鶏鞍　阿奴哩杏　雅鳥安

Purely denotative transcription: 雅土利亜人 = an
Adrian, *adoria jin*

Phonetic & eulogistic transcription: 営鳥庵 = a vacation home run
by birds; 英土梨杏 = English pears and apricots; 鋭度利案 = an
extremely clever plan; 英土里杏 = English apricots; 永鳥庵 = an
eternal bird's hermitage; 雅鳥庵 = an elegant bird's hermitage

Attention-getting transcription: 鴉鳥暗 = a crow in the dark; 婀取
杏 = a beautiful apricot-picker.

Agnes
(f) French, Latin, Greek, "pure, chaste" (LDWG)

Kana transcription: アグネス／あぐねす

Purely phonetic transcription: 阿具値酢　亜偶音州
雅遇値巣　婀紅根諏　椏具襴寿

Purely denotative transcription: 純潔 = pure, *junketsu*; 清
純 = pure, *seijun*; 貞節 = chaste, *teisetsu*; 貞淑 = chaste, *teishuku*;
貞実 = chaste, *teijitsu*

Phonetic & denotative transcription: 婀具根素 = a beauty endowed
with qualities of pureness or untainted simplicity.

Phonetic & eulogistic transcription: 雅遇寧主 = a hostess who
treats her guests elegantly; 婀具音周 = a beauty having a far-
reaching voice; 婀具根寿 = a long-lived beautiful woman; 婀紅
根簾 ; a beauty sitting behind a blind made of red roots (hence a
noble lady). Note: Japanese medieval emperors used to sit behind a
thin rattan blind through which their subjects could only dimly see
their faces.

Attention-getting transcription: 蛙愚寝巣 = a stupid frog sleeping
in the nest.

Al (m) Diminutive of Albert; see Albert

Kana transcription: アル／ある

Purely phonetic transcription: 亜流　雅留　堊瑠 鴉流　阿留 and also 在　有

Purely denotative transcription: See Albert

Phonetic & eulogistic transcription: 雅琉 = an elegant gem; 雅留 = one who stays elegant; 我留 = I stay; 雅流 = an elegant way; 亜流 = an Asian way; 或 = a certain man; 有 = existence.

Attention-getting transcription: 鴉流 = a crow's way; 唖漏 = a faintly audible bird's call.

Alan (m) Celtic, "comely or fair"; "harmony" (ECS)

Kana transcription: アラン／あらん

Purely phonetic transcription: 亜欄　阿卵　雅覧 婀乱　椏嵐　堊藍　蛙浪　或欄　雅蘭

Purely denotative transcription: 美男 = a handsome man, *binan*; 好男子 = a handsome man, *kodanshi*; 美男子 = a handsome man, *binanshi*; 色男 = a handsome man, *irootoko* or 調和 = harmony, *chowa*; 一致 = harmony/agreement, *icchi*; 和合 = harmony, *wago*.

Phonetic and denotative transcription: 雅覧 = one who looks elegant = hence "comely or fair" or 唖良運 = one who smiles at good luck, hence "harmony."

Phonetic & eulogistic transcription: 亜嵐 = an Asian storm; 雅蘭 = a Dutch orchid; 雅藍 = elegant dark blue; 阿乱 = African rebellion; 雅闌 = someone with extreme elegance.

Attention-getting transcription: 蛙乱 = a rebelling frog; 鴉藍 = a caged crow.

Brainteaser: 不在 = does not exist. Note: "Alan" phonetically corresponds to 在らん in Japanese meaning "does not exist."

Albert

(m) Old German, compound of "noble" and "bright" (EGW)

Kana transcription: アルバート ; あるばーと

Purely phonetic transcription: 亜流馬阿徒　或場雅兎有羽阿都　阿留芭亜杜 and also 在婆途　雅留鳩塋瑠場阿戸　鴉流羽亜途 and also 或鳩

Purely denotative transcription: 貴煌 = noble and bright, *kiko*; 貴昭 = noble and bright, *kisho*; 貴燦 = noble and bright, *kisan*; 貴輝 = noble and bright, *kiki*

Phonetic and denotative transcription: 雅婁磨痕 = the bright evidence of frequent polishing, hence "bright."

Phonetic & eulogistic transcription: 或馬雅人 = a certain elegant horse-dealer; 亜流馬阿途 = an Asian horse on the way to Africa; 雅瑠磨人 = an elegant gem polisher; 我留芭雅杜 = I stay in an elegant, flower-filled forest; 亜流鳩 = an Asian dove.

Attention-getting transcription: 或魔討 = one who attacks a demon; 蛙留罵吐 = A frog which shouts words of condemnation; 雅留馬屠 = an elegant horse butcher.

Alex

(m) Pet form of Alexander (LDWG); see Alexander

Kana transcription: アレックス／あれっくす

Purely phonetic transcription: 阿例句酢　亜霊句州雅令玖珠　荒楠　有久寿　荒区巣

Purely denotative transcription: See Alexander

Phonetic and denotative transcription: 雅怜救守 = a elegant and clever defender = hence a "defender of men."

Phonetic & eulogistic transcription: 阿令究守 = an African law researcher; 亜礼共主 = a host with Asian courtesy; 雅励公寿 = an elegant duke who encourages elderly people.

Attention-getting transcription: 阿霊宮巣 = an African ghost in the nest; 亜齢句手 = an old Asian poet.

Alexander
(m) Greek, "defender of man" (EGW)

Kana transcription: アレクサンダー／あれくさんだー

Purely phonetic transcription: 阿例救参堕阿
亜霊駆散駄阿　雅令究参妥阿　荒救讃打噫

Purely denotative transcription: 守護者 = a defending man, *shugosha*; 護衛者 = a defending man, *goeisha*; 庇護者 = a defending man, *higosha*.

Phonetic & denotative transcription: 阿霊救参舵雅 = one who participates in elegantly guiding and saving African souls = hence a "defending man"; 荒救参妥阿 = one who agrees to participate in saving Africans from violence = hence a "defending man."

Phonetic & eulogistic transcription: 阿令救讃妥雅 = a leader who elegantly agrees, praises and saves African laws; 雅礼究算妥 = one who agrees to study about elegant manners; 雅嶺宮参陀 = one who visits an elegant shrine on the ridge to worship Buddha.

Attention-getting transcription: 阿霊宮参妥 = one who agrees to pay a visit to an African ghost's palace; 鴉霊供参蛇雅 ; an elegant snake which pays homage to the crow's spirit.

Alexandra
(f) Feminine form of Alexander (LDWG); see Alexander

Kana transcription: アレグサンドラ／あれさんどら

Purely phonetic transcription: 阿麗公燦度等
亜礼究讃努螺　雅令功残奴裸

Purely denotative transcription: See Alexander.

Phonetic & denotative transcription: 雅励救参度等 = one who tries to save people elegantly = a "defending man."

Phonetic & eulogistic transcription: 阿令救参努良 = one who comes and tries hard to save African laws; 雅礼究残導等 = the last leaders who seek to retain elegance and courtesy; 雅嶺宮参奴等 = people who pay a visit to the shrine on the elegant ridge.

Attention-getting transcription: 阿霊宮残導等 = one who guides to the remains of an African ghost's palace; 鴉霊究残洞裸 = A crow's spirit that seeks to remain in a cave, naked.

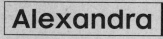

Alfred
(m) Old English, compound of "old" and "great," meaning "counsel" (EGW)

Kana transcription: アルフレッド／あるふれっど

Phonetic transcription: 亜留布霊度　阿瑠譜令土　雅流付礼努　有振度　或触怒

Denotative transcription: 大弁護人 = a great barrister, *daibengonin*; 大助言 = great advice, *daijogen*.

Phonetic & denotative transcription: 有輔励努 = a certain person who makes efforts to help and encourage (people) = hence "counsel"; 雅留父励奴 = a good father who encourages slaves = hence "counsel."

Phonetic and eulogistic transcription: 亜流夫礼努 = a husband who tries to be polite in an Asian manner; 或父励努 = an encouraging father; 有富礼度 = a one who is rich and courteous.

Attention-getting transcription: 或腐霊怒 = a certain rotten angry spirit; 或怖隷奴 = a certain fearful slave; 蛙留豊麗土 = a frog staying in a rich beautiful land.

Alice
(f) Old French, "of noble kind" (LDWG)

Kana transcription: アリス／ありす

Phonetic transcription: 雅理子　亜利州　阿李簾　蛙利寿　蟻酢　蟻洲　有巣

Denotative transcription: 貴族 = a noble family, *kizoku*; 貴人 = a noble person, *kijin*; 華族 = a noble family, *kazoku*; 皇族 = imperial family, *kozoku*; 高族 = a noble family, *kozoku*.

Phonetic & denotative transcription: 雅利子 = an elegant and clever child = hence "of noble kind"; 雅理素 = elegant, intelligent and pure; 雅麗子 = an elegant child.

Phonetic & eulogistic transcription: 亜麗子 = an elegant Asian child; 婀利寿 = a long-lived and clever beauty.

Attention-getting transcription: 亜狸守 = an Asian badger keeper; 蟻巣 = an ant in the nest; 蛙里主 = boss of frog land; 蟻寿 = a long-living ant; 阿狸巣 = an African badger in the nest.

Alison
(f) A pet name for Alice (EGW); see Alice

Kana transcription: アリソン／ありそん
Phonetic transcription: 阿利寸　亜里寸 or 雅利噂
蛙利存　蟻孫　蟻尊　有村
Denotative transcription:　see Alice

Phonetic & denotative transcription:　雅礼孫 = an elegant and courteous grandson = hence "of noble kind"; 雅礼存 = one endowed with elegance and courtesy = hence "of noble kind."

Phonetic and eulogistic transcription:　雅理尊 = elegant, intelligent and respected; 雅利孫 = an elegant and clever grandson; 亜利孫 = a clever Asian grandson.

Attention-getting transcription:　蟻孫 = an ant's grandchild; 蟻餐 = an ant having dinner; 蛙離村 = a frog which leaves a village.

Amanda
(f) Latin, "fit to be loved" (LDWG)

Kana transcription: アマンダ／あまんだ
Phonetic transcription: 亜万打　阿慢惰　雅満駄
蛙鰻田　雅蔓妥　亜漫陀
Denotative transcription:　可愛 = fit to be loved, *kawai*; 愛子 = a lovable girl, *aiko*; 愛児 = a beloved child, *aiji*; 愛嬢 = a beloved daughter, *aijo*; 愛妻 = a beloved wife, *aisai*; 愛妾 = a beloved mistress, *aisho*.

Phonetic & denotative transcription:　愛満陀 = a Buddha who is full of love = hence "fit to be loved"; 婀満兌 = a beauty who is full of delight = hence "fit to be loved."

Phonetic and eulogistic transcription:　雅満陀 = a Buddha who is filled with elegance; 雅曼娜 = an elegant beauty; 雅万雫 = ten thousand elegant dew drops.

Attention-getting transcription:　蛙瞞娜 = a beauty who deceives, but satisfies a frog; 鴉満娜 = a crow which pleases a beauty; 雅鰻田 = an elegant eel in the rice field.

Andrea

(f) Feminine form of Andrew (LDGW); see Andrew

Kana transcription: アンドレア／あんどれあ

Purely phonetic transcription: 案度麗唖　安堵嶺阿　庵土霊亜　按努励雅　鞍奴礼亜　杏土鈴阿

Purely denotative transcription: See Andrew

Phonetic & denotative transcription: 闇怒霊阿 = an angry African ghost in the dark = hence "manly"; 鞍努領雅 = a hardworking president who sits elegantly in the saddle = "manly."

Phonetic & eulogistic transcription: 案努領婀 = a female president who works at making plans; 安導嶺婀 = a beautiful mountain guide; 杏土麗婀 = an elegant beauty in the apricot land; 陰努怜婀 = a clever beauty who labors surreptitiously.

Attention-getting transcription: 鞍怒零雅 = to be inelegantly angry in the saddle; 安堵霊婀 = a beauty's spirit at rest.

Brainteaser: 及怜婀 = and a clever beauty. Note: "And-" = 及 in Japanese. Hence it is read "Andrea."

Andrew

(m) Greek, "manly" (GRS)

Kana transcription: アンドリュウ／あんどりゅう

Purely phonetic transcription: 案度流　安堵柳　庵土粒　按努粒　鞍奴隆　杏土隆

Purely denotative transcription: 男伊達 = manly, *otokodate*; 勇侠 manly, *yukyo*; 侠気 = manly, *kyoki*

Phonetic & denotative transcription: 闇怒龍 = an angry dragon in the dark"; 鞍恫龍 = a threatening dragon in the saddle = "manly."

Phonetic & eulogistic transcription: 案努隆 = one who tries to make a prosperous plan; 安度隆 = a high degree of stability; 杏土隆 = one who is prosperous in the apricot land; 安堵龍 = a dragon at rest.

Attention-getting transcription: 鞍奴笠 = a fellow in the saddle with a bamboo hat.

Brainteaser: 及龍 = and a dragon. Note: "And" = 及 in Japanese and "-rew" corresponds to 龍 in Japanese. Hence it is read "Andrew."

Andy

(m) Diminutive of Andrew (LDWG); see Andrew

Kana transcription: アンデイ／あんでい
Purely phonetic transcription: 案出意　鞍弟伊
庵出位　行出依　案泥　安襧　按祢　鞍出意
杏弟偉　餡泥　晏弟衣

Purely denotative transcription: See Andrew

Phonetic & denotative transcription: 行出威 = to go out to threaten = hence "manly"; 鞍弟偉 = a great brother in the saddle = hence "manly"; 闇出医 = a doctor who goes out in the dark (to cure a patient) = hence "manly."

Phonetic & eulogistic transcription: 案出委 = a committee member who gives suggestions; 安出医 = a doctor who relieves (a patient's) anxiety; 闇出位 = one who goes from obscurity to a high position.

Attention-getting transcription: 鞍泥 = a muddy saddle; 庵泥 = a muddy vacation home; 鴉雲出移 = a crow moving out of a cloud.

Angela

(f) Greek, Latin, "messenger"; "angel" (LDWG)

Kana transcription: アンジェラ／あんじぇら
Purely phonetic transcription: 按辞等　暗示羅
安字羅　行児等　暗仕螺　杏示羅　鞍持裸
案時喇　晏地蘿　餡児等

Purely denotative transcription: 使者 = a messenger, *shisha*; 天使 = an angel, *tenshi*.

Phonetic & denotative transcription: 案示良 = one who guides well = hence a "messenger"; 案児裸 = a naked child who guides = hence an "angel"; 安慈裸 = peaceful, benevolent and naked = an "angel."

Phonetic & eulogistic transcription: 按侍等 = samurai in charge of inspection; 案辞良 = one who is skilled at giving verbal guidance = hence a good interpreter; 鞍侍良 = a samurai who is good at horse-riding = a chivalry; 案示喇 = one who signals by trumpeting = a trumpeter; 案慈良 = one who makes good benevolent propositions.

Attention-getting transcription; 安示喇 = an trumpet which shows safety; 安値螺 = a cheap shell; 暗示喇 = a guiding trumpet.

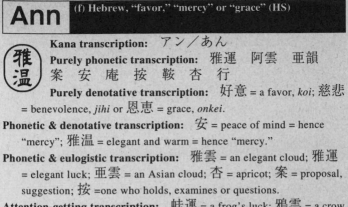

Ann

(f) Hebrew, "favor," "mercy" or "grace" (HS)

Kana transcription: アン／あん

Purely phonetic transcription: 雅運　阿雲　亜韻
案　安　庵　按　鞍　杏　行

Purely denotative transcription: 好意 = a favor, *koi*; 慈悲
= benevolence, *jihi* or 恩恵 = grace, *onkei*.

Phonetic & denotative transcription: 安 = peace of mind = hence
"mercy"; 雅温 = elegant and warm = hence "mercy."

Phonetic & eulogistic transcription: 雅雲 = an elegant cloud; 雅運
= elegant luck; 亜雲 = an Asian cloud; 杏 = apricot; 案 = proposal,
suggestion; 按 =one who holds, examines or questions.

Attention-getting transcription: 蛙運 = a frog's luck; 鴉雲 = a crow
in the cloud; 鮟 = a catfish; 闇 = darkness.

Anna

(f) Greek and Latin form of Hebrew Hannah
(LDWG); see Ann

Kana transcription: アンナ／あんな

Purely phonetic transcription: 案名　杏奈　按名
安名　行那　鞍納　庵菜

Purely denotative transcription: See Ann

Phonetic & denotative transcription: 雅温娜 = an elegant mild =
hence "mercy"; 安納 = one who offers peace = hence "mercy"

Phonetic & eulogistic transcription: 案娜 = a beautiful woman
guide; 杏娜 = a woman with the beauty of an apricot; 鞍娜 = a
beauty in the saddle; 庵娜 = a beauty at her vacation home.

Attention-getting transcription: 雅運娜 = a beauty who has elegant
luck; 闇娜 = a beauty in the dark; 暗奈 = dark hell.

Brainteaser: 壱菜 = a vegetable; 壱名 = a person; 壱難 = a
difficult thing. Note: "An" (= indefinite article) = 壱 (meaning one)
in Japanese. Hence they are read "Anna."

Anthony (m) Latin, "inestimable"; "strength" (ECS)

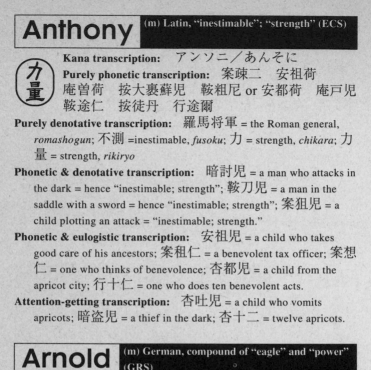

Kana transcription: アンソニ／あんそに

Purely phonetic transcription: 案疎二　安祖荷
庵曽荷　按大裏蘚児　鞍粗尼 or 安都荷　庵戸児
鞍途仁　按徒丹　行途爾

Purely denotative transcription: 羅馬将軍 = the Roman general, *romashogun*; 不測 =inestimable, *fusoku*; 力 = strength, *chikara*; 力量 = strength, *rikiryo*

Phonetic & denotative transcription: 暗討児 = a man who attacks in the dark = hence "inestimable; strength"; 鞍刀児 = a man in the saddle with a sword = hence "inestimable; strength"; 案狙児 = a child plotting an attack = "inestimable; strength."

Phonetic & eulogistic transcription: 安祖児 = a child who takes good care of his ancestors; 案租仁 = a benevolent tax officer; 案想仁 = one who thinks of benevolence; 杏都児 = a child from the apricot city; 行十仁 = one who does ten benevolent acts.

Attention-getting transcription: 杏吐児 = a child who vomits apricots; 暗盗児 = a thief in the dark; 杏十二 = twelve apricots.

Arnold (m) German, compound of "eagle" and "power" (GRS)

Kana transcription: アーノルド／あーのるど

Purely phonetic transcription: 亜阿之琉土　雅阿乗土
阿雅栖瑠奴　蛙亜野漏土　噫脳流度　噫留土噫
載度　噫騎奴 and also 亜之琉土　雅栖瑠奴

Purely denotative transcription: 鷲力 = an eagle's power, *juriki*.

Phonetic & denotative transcription: 阿鴉能留度 = an African crow with a high degree of power.

Phonetic & eulogistic transcription: 噫雅騎努 = a surprised, but elegant and diligent knight; 雅亜騎怒 = an angry, but elegant Asian knight; 雅納瑠度 = one who often offers elegant gems.

Attention-getting transcription: 阿蛙載度 = one who often rides on an African frog; 蛙載奴 = a guy carrying a frog.

Arthur
(m) Celtic, "bear"; Irish, "stone" (EGW)

Kana transcription: アーサー／あーさー

Purely phonetic transcription: 阿雅差雅　亜阿查阿
雅亜沙阿　亜阿鎖雅　噫差亜　噫鎖亜 and also
阿差　亜查　雅沙　阿差　朝雅　麻亜朝

Purely denotative transcription: 熊石 = a bear and a stone, *kumaishi*;
石熊 = a stone bear, *ishikuma*.

Phonetic & denotative transcription: 亜優砂雅 = elegant Asian
sand = hence a (small) "stone"; 雅砂 = elegant sand = a small stone.

Phonetic & eulogistic transcription: 噫查雅 = an elegant inspector;
噫作雅 = Oh, elegant manners; 朝雅 = an elegant morning.

Attention-getting transcription: 阿蛙詐雅 = an African frog's
excellent cheating; 亜蛙嗟噫 = an Asian frog's sigh; 雅鴉查噫 =
an elegant crow's inspection; 阿鴉詐噫 = an African crow's trick.

Brainteaser: 中世英王 = a medieval English king, pronounced
chuseieio.

Audrey
(f) Old English, "noble-strength" (GRS)

Kana transcription: オードリイ／おーどりい

Purely phonetic transcription: 皇努令　欧土嶺
追度玲　旺弩霊　王怒礼　桜奴鈴　鴨土麗

Purely denotative transcription: 貴力 = noble-strength,
kiryoku; 華力 = noble family-power, *karyoku*; 高貴力 = noble
strength, *kokiryoku*; 貴族勢力 = noble's forces, *kizoku seiryoku*.

Phonetic & denotative transcription: 王度令 = frequent royal orders
= hence "noble-strength"; 皇努励 = royal effort encouraged = hence
"noble-bright"; 負奴怜 = wise enough to defeat people = hence
"noble-strength."

Phonetic & eulogistic transcription: 皇能令 = an emperor skilled in
law; 王道礼 = a courteous king.

Attention-getting transcription: 殴奴霊 = a slave-beating ghost; 鴨
度礼 = a courteous wild duck.

Barbara

(f) Greek, "a stranger" (HS)

Kana transcription: バーバラ／ばーばら

Purely phonetic transcription: 馬亜馬等　瑪雅磨羅
婆芭鑼　場蛙魔喇　羽雅碆螺　婆薔薇 and also
馬場等　瑪磨羅　婆芭鑼　場魔喇　羽碆螺

Purely denotative transcription: 部外者 = a stranger, *bugaisha*; 他
人 = a stranger, *tanin*; 不案内者 = a stranger, *fuannai-sha*; 客人
= a guest person, *kyaku-jin*; 異国人 = a stranger, *ikoku-jin*.

Phonetic & denotative transcription: 磨薔薇 = a refined rose (which
is not found locally) = hence a "stranger"; 羽薔薇 = a feather-like
rose = hence a "stranger" (a strange kind of rose not found locally);
婆罵裸 = a old woman who is shouting in the nude = a "stranger."

Phonetic & eulogistic transcription: 芭薔薇 = a rose; 馬場鑼 = the
gong at a stable; 芭磨良 = a good refined flower.

Attention-getting transcription: 婆蛙罵裸 = an old female frog
shouting in the nude; 馬唖婆蝸 = a horse laughing at an old snail.

Barry

(m) Irish, derivative of a word meaning "spear" (EGW)

Kana transcription: バーリイ／ばーりい

Purely phonetic transcription: 馬亜理意　場阿利委
芭猗離異　瑪雅里医 and also 馬理意　場利委

Purely denotative transcription: 槍 = a spear, *yari*; 投槍 =
throwing spear, *nage yari*; 手槍 = a hand spear, *te yari*; 長槍 = a
long spear, *naga yari*; 鎗 = a spear, *yari*.

Phonetic & denotative transcription: 馬猗槍 = one who has a spear
on a horse = a "spear"; 磨雅鎗 = one who polishes an elegant spear.

Phonetic & eulogistic transcription: 馬雅悧医 = a clever and
elegant horse doctor; 瑪猗麗 = one who deals with elegant agates;
磨礼 = someone with polished elegance.

Attention-getting transcription: 魔亜蟻 = an evil Asian ant; 罵阿
蟻 = a shouting African ant; 魔霊 = a evil spirit.

Benjamin

(m) Hebrew, "son of my right hand"; "son of the south" (ECS)

Kana transcription: ベンジャミン／べんじゃみん

Purely phonetic transcription: 弁者明　便蛇眠
便邪岷　鞭社愍　勉砂泯

Purely denotative transcription: 片腕息子 = son of the single hand, *kataude musuko*; 便用息子 = a useful son, *benyo-musuko*; 南部息子 = son of the south, *nanbu musuko*.

Phonetic & denotative transcription: 便者民 = a useful man = hence "son of my right hand"; 便助民 = a useful helper = hence "son of my right hand."

Phonetic & eulogistic transcription: 弁者民 = lawyers; 勉者民 = industrious people; 鞭者民 = one who encourages people.

Attention-getting transcription: 鞭蛇眠 = one who whips a sleeping snake; 勉邪民 = those who disturb studying; 勉者眠 = a sleeping scholar.

Bernard

(m) Old German, compound of "a bear" and "stern" (EGW)

Kana transcription: バーナード／ばーなーど

Purely phonetic transcription: 馬雅菜亜度　芭娜努
罵亜名阿土　場雅那亜道　魔阿奈雅奴
芭亜娜雅努 and also 馬菜度　罵名土　場那藤

Purely denotative transcription: 大熊 = a big bear, *okuma*; 荒熊 = a ferocious bear, *areguma*; 狂暴熊 = an untamed bear, *kyobo guma*.

Phonetic & denotative transcription: 魔穴怒 = a roaring devil in the cave = hence "a bear", "stern."

Phonetic & eulogistic transcription: 馬雅菜亜土 = An elegant horse in an Asian vegetable field; 馬雅名導 = one who guides beautiful horses.

Attention-getting transcription: 罵蛙難唖度 = a shouting frog which often has difficulty laughing; 魔唖娜度 = a demon which often smiles at beautiful girls.

Bert (m) Pet form of Albert (WFWG); see Albert

Kana transcription: バート／ばーと
Purely phonetic transcription: 馬雅登　磨亜度
罵阿頭　魔唖都　場唖妬　芭雅杜　羽蛙図
婆阿鍍 and also 馬登　磨度　罵頭　魔都

Purely denotative transcription: See Albert

Phonetic & denotative transcription: 磨雅頭 = one who hones his or her mind elegantly = hence, "bright."

Phonetic & eulogistic transcription: 芭雅納 = one who supplies elegant flowers = hence, a flower dealer; 羽雅頭 = one whose head is decorated with beautiful feathers = hence an Indian chief; 瑪亜杜 = a forest where Asian agate is produced.

Attention-getting transcription: 慕亜頭 = the head of Asian toads; 馬唖度 = a frequently laughing horse; 馬蛙妬 = a horse which is jealous of a frog.

Bertha (f) A Teutonic name meaning "shining" (HS)

Kana transcription: バーサ／ばーさ
Purely phonetic transcription: 馬亜砂　場阿差
羽雅左　芭蛙作　魔雅紗　瑪娜査　磨噫瑳 and
also 馬砂　場差　羽左　芭作

Purely denotative transcription: 光輝 = shining, *koki*; 光射 = shining, *kosha*; 晃耀 = shining, *koyo*; 輝耀 = shining, *kiyo*; 光晃 = shining, *koko*.

Phonetic & denotative transcription: 磨雅鎖 = to polish the elegant chain = hence "bright, shining."

Phonetic & eulogistic transcription: 馬雅作 = one who makes horses elegant = a horse trainer; 瑪雅瑳 = one who polishes agate elegantly = hence an agate polisher; 芭亜査 = a researcher of Asian flowers.

Attention-getting transcription: 婆蛙鎖 = a chained old female frog; 魔鴉嗟 = a lamenting devilish crow.

34

Betty (f) Pet form of Elizabeth (LDWG); see Elizabeth

Kana transcription: ベテイ／べてい

Purely phonetic transcription: 辺手偉　琶帝　部堤
琶庭　米帝　部廷　琶廷

Purely denotative transcription: See Elizabeth

Phonetic & denotative transcription: 瞑定意 = the will to die = "oath of God"; 迷諦慰 = to console someone troubled by denunciation = hence "oath of God."

Phonetic & eulogistic transcription: 米帝 = the American empress; 部帝 = the empress of the tribe; 琶打 = a Japanese mandolin player; 魅貞 = one who is charming and chaste; 美偵 = a beautiful female detective.

Attention-getting transcription: 迷帝 = a wavering empress; 謎鵜 = a mysterious cormorant; 謎帝 = a mysterious empress.

Bill (m) Pet form of William (LDWG); see William

Kana transcription: ビル／びる

Purely phonetic transcription: 魅婁　美留　毘留
魅瑠　琶瑠　比流　備瑠

Purely denotative transcription: See William

Phonetic & denotative transcription: 備意留 = one who is endowed with a strong will = hence "will and helmet"; 魅意留 = one who has a charming will = hence "will and helmet."

Phonetic & eulogistic transcription: 美威留 = one who stays handsome and dignified; 魅流 = one with effluent charm; 鼻威留 = one whose nose stays dignified; 眉医留 = an optometrist.

Attention-getting transcription: 肥留 = one who is fat; 鼻漏 = a runny nose; 尾流 = a flowing tail.

Brainteaser: 建物 = a building. Note: "Bill" (= Buil., building abbreviated) = 建物 in Japanese. Hence it is read "Bill."

Bob
(m) Pet form of Robert (LDWG); see Robert

望豊

Kana transcription: ボブ／ぼぶ

Purely phonetic transcription: 慕鵡　母輔　慕武
暮務　菩奉　模舞　簿部

Purely denotative transcription: See Robert

Phonetic & denotative transcription: 望豊 = to appear promising = hence "bright"; 模武 = a model samurai = hence "famous, bright."

Phonetic & eulogistic transcription: 膨豊 = expanding riches; 坊豊 = a rich priest; 慕武 = a samurai who is longed for by people.

Attention-getting transcription: 忘鵡 = a forgetful parrot; 望無 = one who is hopeless; 暴鵡 = a violent parrot; 肪武 = a fat samurai.

Brenda
(f) Probably from Old Norse, meaning "sword" (LDWG)

刀剣

Kana transcription: ブレンダ／ぶれんだ

Purely phonetic transcription: 部連舵　武廉妥
豊恋兒　舞練打　歩簾駄

Purely denotative transcription: 剣 = a sword, *ken*; 刀 = a sword, *katana*; 刀剣 = a sword, *token*; 紫電 = a sword, *shiden*; 秋水 = a sword, *shusui*.

Phonetic & denotative transcription: 武連打 = a samurai who beats (enemies) repeatedly (with his sword) = hence a "sword."

Phonetic & eulogistic transcription: 舞連蛇 = a continuously dancing snake; 負連打 = one who continuously beats down (enemies); 務練舵 = one in charge of training and guiding = hence an educator.

Attention-getting transcription: 撫恋蛇 = one who caresses a beloved snake; 務練蛇 = a snake tamer; 舞恋陀 = a dancing Buddha who is in love.

Brian

(m) British or Irish, "hill" (EGW)

Kana transcription: ブライアン／ぶらいあん

Purely phonetic transcription: 歩等医案　武鑼異暗
部裸委安　蒲喇偉杏　撫来闇　負雷庵　不來按

Purely denotative transcription: 丘 = hill, *oka*; 岡 = hill,
oka; 丘陵 = hill, *kyuryo*; 丘岡 = hill, *kyuko*; 岡陵 = hill, *koryo*;
小山 = hill, *koyama*.

Phonetic & denotative transcription: 霧来安 = a peaceful foggy
place = hence a "hill."

Phonetic & eulogistic transcription: 武来闇 = a samurai who comes
in the dark; 負雷庵 = a lightning-proof vacation home; 舞雷雅雲
= a elegant dancing lightning cloud.

Attention-getting transcription: 葡頼案 = a plan made thanks to
wine; 舞騾食杏 = a dancing mule which eats apricots; 豊蝸移庵
= a rich snail which moves to a vacation home.

Bridget

(m) Celtic, "strength" (ECS)

Kana transcription: ブリジット／ぶりじっと

Purely phonetic transcription: 部離辞戸　武里辞渡
歩悧示都　不理時登　舞利次図　豊裏治都

Purely denotative transcription: 力 = strength, *chikara* or
tsutomu; 力量 = strength, *rikiryou*; 能力 = strength, ability,
noryoku; 勢力 = power, *seiryoku*; 実力 = power, *kitsuryoku*.

Phonetic & denotative transcription: 負理示妬 = jealousy proves to
beat reason = jealousy makes man do evil = hence "strength"; 武理
慈頭 = an intelligent and benevolent samurai chief = "strength."

Phonetic & eulogistic transcription: 武理慈図 = a samurai who
shows reason and benevolence; 舞麗尼頭 = a chief nun who dances
elegantly.

Attention-getting transcription: 鵡狸示妬 = a parrot which shows
jealousy to a badger; 撫狸尼度 = a nun who often pets a badger.

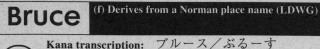

Bruce (f) Derives from a Norman place name (LDWG)

Kana transcription: ブルース／ぶるーす

Purely phonetic transcription: 舞琉雨諏　撫留宇州
部瑠右巣 and also 舞琉諏　撫留州　部瑠巣

Purely denotative transcription: 西仏都市 = a West
French city, *seifutsu toshi*.

Phonetic & denotative transcription: 仏留州 = a state
which lies in France = hence "a Norman place."

Phonetic & eulogistic transcription: 武留有寿 = a samurai who
enjoys longevity; 武流優司 = a chief with proficiency in the
martial arts; 豊留主 = a rich master; 務瑠守 = one who is in
charge of keeping gems.

Attention-getting transcription: 霧流烏巣 = a crow in a nest
flowing in the mist; 鸚留鵜巣 = a parrot which stays in a
cormorant's nest.

Carl (m) Germanic, "man," especially "countryman, husbandman" (LDWG)

Kana transcription: カール／かーる

Purely phonetic transcription: 家阿留　華雅瑠
加亜琉　香雅鏤　歌阿流 and also 家留　華瑠
加琉　香有　花在

Purely denotative transcription: 男 = a man, *otoko*; 男児 = a man,
danji; 田舎男 = a countryman, *inakaotoko*; 田舎者 = a
countryman, *inakamono*; 農夫 = a farmer, *nofu*; 百姓 = a
husbandman, *hyakusho*.

Phonetic & denotative transcription: 瓜猗留 = one who gathers
melons = hence a "countryman, husbandman"; 嫁有 = a bride-owner
= hence a "man"; 加婀瑠 = one who gives gems to a pretty woman
= a "man."

Phonetic & eulogistic transcription: 家有 = a house owner; 嘉有留
= one who owns happiness; 歌有 = a singer; 価有 = a valuable man.

Attention-getting transcription: 嫁蛙留 = a frog bride; 駕蛙留 =
one who rides on a frog = a frog rider; 鹿雅留 = an elegant deer.

Carla
(f) Feminine form of Carl (LDWG); see Carl

Kana transcription: カーラ／かーら

Purely phonetic transcription: 歌雅等　香亜良　嫁阿羅　華哇蘿　誇婀蝸

Purely denotative transcription: See Carl

Phonetic & denotative transcription: 駕雅騾 = one who rides on a mule skillfully = hence a "man, farmer."

Phonetic & eulogistic transcription: 霞雅蝸 = a snail in the elegant mist; 花雅良 = a good and elegant flower; 誇雅裸 = one who is proud of her nudity = hence a nude model.

Attention-getting transcription: 鹿唖騾 = a deer who laughs at a mule; 華蛙良 = a good and brilliant frog in the nude.

Carol
(f) Pet form of Caroline (LDWG); meaning "man"; "song of joy" (ECS)

Kana transcription: キャロル／きゃろる

Purely phonetic transcription: 喜野路瑠　輝耶露留　気哉侶流　記夜呂瑠　貴矢蕗硫　希弥炉琉

Purely denotative transcription: 男 = a man, *otoko*; 男性 = a man, *dansei*; 男子 = a man, *danshi* 紳士 = a man, *shinshi* or 喜乃歌 = a song of joy, *yorokobi-no-uta*; 歓喜乃歌 = a song of joy, *kanki-no-uta*; 喜悦乃歌 = a song of joy, *kietsu-no-uta*.

Phonetic & denotative transcription: 騎野路留 = a knight on the country road = hence a "man"; 嬉屋朗漏 = joy and cheers which come out of the room = hence "song of joy."

Phonetic & eulogistic transcription: 貴冶慮留 = a sexy and considerate noble; 嬉夜路漏 = nocturnal merriment faintly audible from the road; 輝野露流 = shining dew drops in the field.

Attention-getting transcription: 鬼家蘆留 = a devil in the reed house; 亀夜浪流 = a nocturnal wave of tortoises; 喜夜旅留 = one who enjoys a happy night.

Caroline
(f) Feminine form of Charles (EGW); see Charles

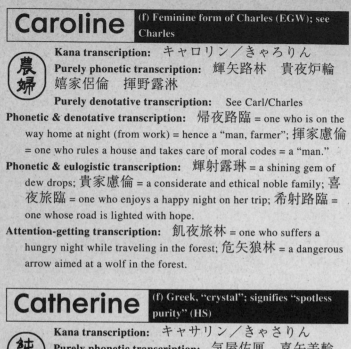

農婦

Kana transcription: キャロリン／きゃろりん

Purely phonetic transcription: 輝矢路林　貴夜炉輪　嬉家侶倫　揮野露淋

Purely denotative transcription: See Carl/Charles

Phonetic & denotative transcription: 帰夜路臨 = one who is on the way home at night (from work) = hence a "man, farmer"; 揮家慮倫 = one who rules a house and takes care of moral codes = a "man."

Phonetic & eulogistic transcription: 輝射露琳 = a shining gem of dew drops; 貴家慮倫 = a considerate and ethical noble family; 喜夜旅臨 = one who enjoys a happy night on her trip; 希射路臨 = one whose road is lighted with hope.

Attention-getting transcription: 飢夜旅林 = one who suffers a hungry night while traveling in the forest; 危矢狼林 = a dangerous arrow aimed at a wolf in the forest.

Catherine
(f) Greek, "crystal"; signifies "spotless purity" (HS)

純白

Kana transcription: キャサリン／きゃさりん

Purely phonetic transcription: 気屋佐厘　喜矢差輪　貴野査林　嬉夜嵯倫　揮哉鎖鈴　輝耶瑳琳　嘉瑳倫　香唆隣　歌差輪

Purely denotative transcription: 水晶 = crystal, *suisho*; 純潔 = purity, *junketsu*; 清純 = clean and pure, *seijun*; 貞潔 = purity, fidelity, *teiketsu*; 純白 = spotless purity, *junpaku*.

Phonetic & denotative transcription: 佳磋琳 = a well-polished gem = "spotless purity"; 佳素倫 = good and moral = "spotless purity."

Phonetic & eulogistic transcription: 輝雅磋鈴 = a brightly polished, elegant bell; 花茶林 = a tea flower in the forest; 佳小鈴 = a good small bell; 嫁作琳 = a bride who makes gems.

Attention-getting transcription: 鬼阿瑳鱗 = the African devil's gem-like scales; 過早醂 = an immature wine; 過査懍 = one who is afraid of scrutiny; 嫁茶淋 = a bride having tea alone.

Cecil (m) Latin, "blind" (HS)

Kana transcription: セシール／せしーる

Purely phonetic transcription: 瀬師偉瑠　背四畏硫
施至威鏤　世資伊留　瀬師瑠　背四硫　世資留
畝詩琉　勢士流　脊知　世識　世汁

Purely denotative transcription: 盲 = blind, *mekura*; 盲人 = a blind
person, *mojin*; 盲目 = blind, *momoku*; 盲者 = a blind person, *moja*;
瞽人 = a blind person, *kojin*.

Phonetic & denotative transcription: 世視異留 = one who sees the
world in a different manner = hence "blind"; 声知 = one who knows
by means of voice = hence "blind."

Phonetic & eulogistic transcription: 施子偉留 = one who makes
children great; 施氏威流 = one who makes the family famous; 勢
至威漏 = one who is dignified, but forceful; 勢氏偉流 = the fame
of the prosperous family is spreading around.

Attention-getting transcription: 背止留 = one whose growth has
stopped = a short person; 瀬死偉流 = the stream which has
drowned a great man.

Cecilia 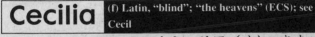 (f) Latin, "blind"; "the heavens" (ECS); see Cecil

Kana transcription: セシーリア／せしーりあ

Purely phonetic transcription: 勢姿流　施偲留
盛知瀬紫婁　世司漏　誠枝瑠

Purely denotative transcription: See Cecil

Phonetic & denotative transcription: 世視痢婀 = a beauty who is
aching to see the world, but cannot = hence "blind"; 正覗離婀 = a
blind beauty = hence "blind."

Phonetic & eulogistic transcription: 世視利婀 = a clever beauty
who sees the world; 清姉麗雅 = a pure and elegant elder sister; 誠
志理婀 = a wise beauty with a sincere will.

Attention-getting transcription: 背脂痢婀 = a beauty who suffers
from a fat back; 妻獅離雅 = an elegant lion wife who is divorced.

Charlene
(f) Feminine form of Charles (LDWG); see Charles

茶雅漣

Kana transcription: チャーレン／ちゃーれん
Purely phonetic transcription: 智野阿連　知哉亜恋
治耶唖練　茶雅漣　茶阿蓮
Purely denotative transcription: See Carl/Charles
Phonetic & denotative transcription: 植野雅蓮 = one
who plants elegant lotuses = hence a "farmer."

Phonetic & eulogistic transcription: 知也婀恋 = an intelligent
beauty in love; 遅夜恋 = love in the late evening; 智婀錬 = a
beauty who improves her intelligence.

Attention-getting transcription: 恥夜恋 = a shameless night love;
痴也憐 = a pitiful idiot; 恥家連 = a row of shameful houses.

Charles
(m) Old German; "a man" (EGW); from a word meaning "man, farmer" (LDWG)

百姓

Kana transcription: チャールズ／ちゃーるず
Purely phonetic transcription: 智野阿瑠図　茶阿婁逗
知哉亜留頭　治耶唖漏杜　茶雅流徒　茶雅瑠豆
Purely denotative transcription: See Carl

Phonetic & denotative transcription: 植野雅留徒 = one who stays
in a beautiful plantation = hence a "man, farmer."

Phonetic & eulogistic transcription: 智家唖婁頭 = an intelligent
master who frequently laughs; 知野瑠図 = one who knows gems in
the field from a chart; 茶雅留杜 = a beautiful tea plant in the
forest; 遅夜留頭 = a boss who stays late at night (in the office); 智
雅漏徒 = one who exudes intelligence and elegance.

Attention-getting transcription: 恥夜留頭 = a boss who remains
shameful at night; 痴也留徒 = an idiot; 恥家留頭 = a boss who
remains in a shameful house.

Charlie
(m) Pet form of Charles (EGW); see Charles

Kana transcription: チャーリー／ちゃーりー
Purely phonetic transcription: 智野阿利意　茶阿吏偉
治耶唖麗威　茶雅璃畏　茶雅里位　智野利意
知哉理医　治耶麗威　茶璃　茶吏

Purely denotative transcription: See Carl/Charles

Phonetic & denotative transcription: 植野雅梨囲 = one who is in a beautiful pear plantation = hence a "man, farmer."

Phonetic & eulogistic transcription: 治家利威 = a clever and dignified person who rules the house; 知野吏位 = an official who knows the field; 茶雅璃威 = a beautiful and dignified brown gem; 遅夜吏位 = an official (working) late at night (in the office); 智雅利威 = one who is intelligent, elegant, clever and dignified.

Attention-getting transcription: 遅夜狸移 = a badger moving late at night; 植野離猪 = a wild boar which leaves the plantation; 治爺離医 = a doctor who leaves to cure an old man.

Charlotte
(f) Italian form of Charles (EGW); see Charles

Kana transcription: シャーロット／しゃーろっと
Purely phonetic transcription: 姐雅露都　謝阿炉登
斜唖路頭　紗雅慮杜　射唖櫨妬　写阿櫓度

Purely denotative transcription: See Carl/Charles

Phonetic & denotative transcription: 者留慮土 = one who takes care of the earth = hence a "farmer."

Phonetic & eulogistic transcription: 射流朗人 = a person who exudes cheer; 写瑠露図 = one who paints misty pictures onto gems; 謝留労頭 = a boss who thanks for labor; 赦留虜逃 = one who permits a slave to run away.

Attention-getting transcription: 姐留魯頭 = a stupid female boss; 邪留略人 = an evil bribing person.

Brainteaser: 車流連中 = those who run the cars = hence taxi drivers. Note: "-lotte" (= lot) = 連中 in Japanese. Hence it is read "Charlotte."

Cheryl

(f) Development from "cherry," first used in the 1920s when Beryl was a popular name (LDWG)

Kana transcription: チリール／ちりーる

Purely phonetic transcription: 知麗位留　智利偉妻 治吏威漏　植梨囲留

Purely denotative transcription: 桜花 = cherry blossoms, *sakura bana*; 桜木 = a cherry tree, *sakuragi*; 桜樹 = a cherry tree, *oju*; 花桜 = a blooming cherry tree, *hana zakura*.

Phonetic & denotative transcription: 植麗偉留 = a plant which stays beautiful and great = hence a "cherry tree."

Phonetic & eulogistic transcription: 智麗偉漏 = one who exudes wisdom, beauty and greatness; 知利威留 = one who is wise, clever and dignified; 持麗違瑠 = an unusually elegant gem.

Attention-getting transcription: 痴狸葦留 = an idiot badger in the reeds; 智零猪留 = a wild boar which has no wisdom at all; 蜘梨 食留 = a spider which eats a pear.

Christina

(f) Means "a follower of Christ" (HS)

Kana transcription: クリスティーナ／くりすてぃーな

Purely phonetic transcription: 駆理蘇手位菜 駈利子帝威名　鳩梨巣廷偉那　紅麗雛呈奈 宮離州庭南　栗守弟畏名

Purely denotative transcription: See Christopher

Phonetic & denotative transcription: 基督畏娜 = a solemn Christian beauty = hence "a follower of Christ."

Phonetic & eulogistic transcription: 究理守貞偉娜 = a great chaste beauty who seeks and keeps truth; 久理寿帝名 = a wise empress whose fame is eternal; 公利寿禎娜 = a duchess who is clever, long-living, chaste and beautiful; 基督医娜 = a beautiful Christian doctor.

Attention-getting transcription: 苦吏主邸名 = a boss of officials in trouble at a famous estate; 紅狸巣邸菜 = a pink badger in a nest made of flowers; 基督威娜 = an arrogant Christian beauty.

Christopher
(m) Greek "one who carries Christ" in his heart (LDWG)

Kana transcription: クリストファー／くりすとふぁー

Purely phonetic transcription: 苦裏巣都夫阿
久哩寿徒賦堊　栗州戸父亜　苦裏巣都夫
究麗諏渡譜　倶悧須途賦　久哩寿徒賦

Purely denotative transcription: 基督者 = a Christian, *kirisuto-sha*; 基督信者 = a Christ believer, *kirisuto shinja*; 基督教徒 = a Christian, *kirisuto kyoto*.

Phonetic & denotative transcription: 基督附猗 = a Christ-bearer = hence "one who carries Christ"; 基督把 = Christ-carrier = hence "one who carries Christ."

Phonetic & eulogistic transcription: 究理守人賦 = one who is obliged to seek the truth; 救痢子人負 = one who saves suffering defeated people; 基督覇 = Christ, who conquers (all); 基督播 = one who spreads Christianity; 基督波 = Christian waves.

Attention-getting transcription: 栗巣吐羽 = a bird vomits chestnuts into its nest; 栗数十破 = one who breaks ten chestnuts.

Chuck
(m) Pet form of Charles (LDWG); see Charles

Kana transcription: チャック／ちゃっく

Purely phonetic transcription: 智野阿宮　知哉亜駈
治耶唖玖　茶雅究　茶阿救　茶雅供　致雅久

Purely denotative transcription: See Carl/Charles

Phonetic & denotative transcription: 茶貢 = one who offers tea = hence a "farmer"; 茶供 = one who supplies tea = hence a "farmer."

Phonetic & eulogistic transcription: 知也公 = a wise duke; 治野救 = one who rules and saves the field; 智雅究 = one who seeks wisdom and elegance.

Attention-getting transcription: 恥蛙紅 = a shameful pink frog; 痴雅公 = an elegant duke who is an idiot; 稚邪狗 = an evil puppy.

Cindy (f) Pet form of Cynthia (LDWG); see Cynthia

Purely phonetic transcription: 真出位　新祢
神弟位　慎出意　信出偉　進襧

Purely denotative transcription:　See Cynthia

Phonetic & denotative transcription: 神出畏 = a solemn
god = hence a "goddess."

Phonetic & eulogistic transcription: 慎出威 = one who is careful
and dignified; 信出移 = one who has come to believe; 進出医 = a
visiting doctor; 清出威 = one who is pure and dignified.

Attention-getting transcription: 新出猪 = a newcomer wild boar; 神
出井 = a god which comes out of the well; 娠出威 = a dignified
pregnant woman.

Clara (f) Latin, "bright, clear" (EGW)

Purely phonetic transcription: 句楽等　久驟等
俱良鑼　究螺等　救裸驟　苦楽楽　九羅等
丘驟等　倉良　蔵羅　鞍裸

Purely denotative transcription: 明 = bright, *akira*; 耀明
= bright, *yomei*; 明燦 = bright, *meisan*; 光輝 = shining, *koki*; 輝耀
= shining, *kiyo*; 明瞭 = clear, *meiryo*; 明快 = clear, *meikai*; 明確
= clear, *meikaku*.

Phonetic & denotative transcription: 空良裸 = a good naked
(cloudless) sky = hence "clear"; 倉裸 = a vacant storage house =
hence "clear"; 孔良裸 = a vacant hole = hence "clear"; 鞍裸 = a
naked saddle = hence "clear."

Phonetic & eulogistic transcription: 救裸等 = one who saves naked
poor people; 駆良驟 = a good mule keeper; 工喇鑼 = a maker of
trumpets and gongs; 貢良羅 = one who offers good thin cloth.

Attention-getting transcription: 紅良驟 = a good pink mule; 公裸
驟 = a duchess on a mule without a saddle; 駈良驟 = a running
mule.

Claude

(m) Latin, presumably deriving from "lame" (LDWG)

跛者

Kana transcription: クロード／くろーど

Purely phonetic transcription: 苦牢奴　句朗土
丘労度　救老弩　究郎怒　倶郎童　久朗啖
苦労努　駆狼度

Purely denotative transcription: 跛 = lame, *chinba* or *bikko*; 跛者 = a lame person, *hisha*; 跛足 = a lame leg, *hisoku*; 片跛 = a lame person, *henpi*; 跛脚 = a lame leg, *hakyaku*; 足蹇 = a lame leg, *sokuken*.

Phonetic & denotative transcription: 苦労度 = often troubled = hence "lame"; 躯労度 = a body which is often troubled = "lame."

Phonetic & eulogistic transcription: 救老奴 = one who saves an old slave; 供労王度 = one who often offers labor to the king; 究朗王努 = a king who makes an effort to seek cheerfulness; 究良努 = one who tries to be good.

Attention-getting transcription: 駆狼奴 = a wolf-hunter; 吼弄殴怒 = to loudly denounce and angrily beat someone; 玖露王土 = a gem-filled kingdom.

Claudia

(f) Feminine form of Claude (EGW); see Claude

Kana transcription: クローデイア／くろーでいあ

Purely phonetic transcription: 苦牢出畏雅　久朗出阿
句朗出位阿　救老出偉雅　究楼出哇　倶瀧出婀

Purely denotative transcription: See Claude

Phonetic & denotative transcription: 苦労出婀 = a beauty who suffers from hardships = hence "lame."

Phonetic & eulogistic transcription: 究朗雄出雅 = one who seeks to be cheerful, heroic and elegant; 公良出威婀 = a beautiful duchess who has become good and dignified; 救労出医雅 = an elegant doctor who saves laborers.

Attention-getting transcription: 狗婁出慰蛙 = a dog which often consoles frogs; 駒婁出唖 = a horse which often laughs.

Claire

(f) Latin, "clear, bright, shining, brilliant"; figuratively "I am renowned, illustrious" (HS)

明燦

Kana transcription: クレール／くれーる

Purely phonetic transcription: 区礼慧留　究霊衛流　倶麗恵鏤　苦礼絵硫　呉意琉　暮位瑠　莫異琉

Purely denotative transcription: 明 = bright, *akira*; 耀明 = bright, *yomei*; 明燦 = bright, *meisan*; 光輝 = shining, *koki*; 輝耀 = shining, *kiyo*; 明瞭 = clear, *meiryo*.

Phonetic & denotative transcription: 供藜留 = to offer clarity = hence "clear"; 貢聆留 = to offer brightness = hence "bright"; 究怜留 = to seek brightness = hence "brilliant."

Phonetic & eulogistic transcription: 公怜偉留 = a great clever duke; 玖麗漏 = a gem of decreasing elegance; 救霊留 = one who saves a spirit; 紅麗瑠 = an elegant pink gem; 苦零恵留 = one blessed without any trouble.

Attention-getting transcription: 暮移留 = twilight; 苦霊居 = a ghost suffering from pain.

Clifford

(m) Common English place name originally referring to a "ford near a slope" (LDWG)

崖津

Kana transcription: クリフォード／くりふぉーど

Purely phonetic transcription: 句理父追度　栗符欧土　久裏賦鴨土　苦利譜皇努　究哩夫翁藤

Purely denotative transcription: 崖津 = a cliff and a ford, *gaketsu*; 崖瀬 = a cliff and a ford, *gakese*; 断崖津 = a cliff and a ford, *dangaitsu*; 嶮崖瀬 = a cliff and a ford, *kengaise*.

Phonetic & denotative transcription: 丘裏怖圧土 = a place behind a hill which causes fear = hence "cliff, ford."

Phonetic & eulogistic transcription: 栗豊王土 = a king in a land rich in chestnuts; 公理富欧土 = a wise, rich duke in Europe; 公吏宝土 = an official in treasure land; 玖里豊土 = a land rich in gems.

Attention-getting transcription: 究離肪努 = one who tries to get rid of fat; 狗理歩王土 = a dog which walks in the kingdom.

Colin

(m) Pet form of Nicholas (LDWG); see Nicholas

皇淋

Kana transcription: コリン／こりん

Purely phonetic transcription: 誇淋　瑚倫　虎輪
湖林　許琳　呼鈴　小麟

Purely denotative transcription: See Nicholas

Phonetic & denotative transcription: 攻利引 = one who attacks to
gain victory = hence "victory, people."

Phonetic & eulogistic transcription: 護倫 = one who upholds ethics;
虹輪 = a rainbow ring; 顧倫 = one who thinks of ethics; 小琳 = a
small gem; 皇淋 = a lonely emperor; 晃輪 = a shining ring.

Attention-getting transcription: 虎淋 = a lonely tiger; 狐林 = a fox
in the forest or a forest fox; 公倫 = an ethical duke; 乎鈴 = a
calling bell.

Connie

(f) Latin, pet form of Constance which means
"holding firmly together" (HS)

光新

Kana transcription: コニー／こにー

Purely phonetic transcription: 后尼威　香丹違
誇仁偉　乎児意　好荷慰　光新

Purely denotative transcription: 不変 = invariable, *fuhen*;
操 = constancy, *misao*; 節操 = constancy, *sesso*; 忠実 = fidelity,
chujitsu; 志操堅固 = consistency, *shisokengo*.

Phonetic & denotative transcription: 固仁維 = to maintain
benevolence firmly = hence "constancy, firmness"; 抗仁移 = to
oppose a departure from benevolence = hence "constancy, firmness."

Phonetic & eulogistic transcription: 誇児偉 = one who is proud of
her great child; 固仁医 = a solidly benevolent doctor; 后認医 = a
doctor appointed by the queen; 公仁威 = a benevolent dignified
duke; 幸尼偉 = a great nun who is happy.

Attention-getting transcription: 虎児異 = a strange tiger cub; 狐丹
威 = a horrifying red fox; 垢児猪 = a dirty wild boar child.

Curtis

(m) A common surname, originating in the nickname "courteous" (EGW)

Kana transcription: カーチス／かーちす

Purely phonetic transcription: 歌亜地酢　香雅知巣
花阿値州　華唖置寿　嘉血守　加恥諏　家千数
課治須　家亜貞州　華艇須　花邸巣　香帝諏

Purely denotative transcription: 礼儀 = courtesy, *reigi*; 儀礼 = courtesy, *girei*; 懇懃 = kind, polite, *ingin*; 丁重 = courteous, *teicho*.

Phonetic & denotative transcription: 加雅丁威主 = a master showing elegance, courtesy and dignity = hence "courteous"; 荷禎以子 = a child endowed with proper manners = "courteous"; 佳雅呈司 = an official showing elegant good manners = "courteous."

Phonetic & eulogistic transcription: 加雅呈素 = one who offers simple elegance; 荷廷枢 = one who is in charge of all court affairs.

Attention-getting transcription: 駕蛙帝子 = an emperor's child riding on a frog; 鹿蛙堤雛 = a deer which gives a frog a fledgling.

Cynthia

(f) Greek, a title of the moon goddess, from Mt. Cynthos on the island of Delos (LDWG)

Kana transcription: シンシア／しんしあ

Purely phonetic transcription: 真士亜　信詩阿
慎師聖　新史猗　審志雅　芯資鴉　心至婀

Purely denotative transcription: 島山 = an island mountain, *shimayama*; 神山 = a divine mountain, *shinzan*; 月乃女神 = moon goddess, *tsuki-no-megami*.

Phonetic & denotative transcription: 神祀婀 = a beautiful woman worshiped as a god = "goddess"; 信史婀 = a beautiful woman of olden times believed by many people = hence "the moon goddess."

Phonetic & eulogistic transcription: 清姿婀 = a beautiful woman of pure appearance; 寝獅雅 = an elegant lion which is asleep; 慎師雅 = an elegant teacher who is careful; 真資雅 = one who has real elegance.

Attention-getting transcription: 伸髭婀 = a girl who has long beard; 娠獅阿 = a pregnant African lioness; 賑脂蛙 = a noisy fat frog.

Cyril
(m) Greek, probably derived from "lord" (EGW)

Kana transcription: シリル／しりる

Purely phonetic transcription: 史里留　市利琉
至俐瑠　資里榎　志麗硫　詩離流　士理留

Purely denotative transcription: 首長 = a lord, head, *shucho*; 支配者 = a ruler, *shihaisha*; 領主 = a lord, *ryoshu*; 統治者 = a ruler, *tochisha*; 男爵 = a baron, *danshaku*; 公爵 = a duke, *koshaku*; 主人 = a master, *shujin*.

Phonetic & denotative transcription: 主利留 = a rich lord = hence a "lord"; 主里留 = a lord who stays in his territory = hence a "lord"; 主理漏 = a lord who shows intelligence = hence a "lord."

Phonetic & eulogistic transcription; 師理留 = a wise teacher; 侍理留 = a wise samurai; 司吏留 = a government official; 紫麗瑠 = an elegant purple gem; 至痢流 = one who gets rid of diseases.

Attention-getting transcription: 髭麗留 = an elegant beard keeper; 脂狸留 = a fat badger; 獅利留 = a clever lion.

Danny
(m) Pet form of Daniel (EGW); see Daniel

Kana transcription: ダニー／だにー

Purely phonetic transcription: 打荷偉　妥仁威
駄弐畏　舵尼慰　陀丹位　兌仁

Purely denotative transcription: See Daniel

Phonetic & denotative transcription: 大仁威 = great dignified benevolence = hence "God has judged."

Phonetic & eulogistic transcription: 陀仁偉 = a Buddha who gives great benevolence; 舵児威 = one who leads kids with dignity; 大児畏 = a big child who is respected; 妥仁偉 = one who nobly compromises out of benevolence.

Attention-getting transcription: 蛇児威 = a fearful snake kid; 打丹猪 = one who beats a red badger; 蛇似 = one who resembles a snake; 惰児猪 = a lazy badger child.

Daniel

(m) Hebrew, "God has judged" (EGW)

Kana transcription: ダニエル／だにえる

Purely phonetic transcription: 打荷江留　妥仁絵流
駄弐恵硫　舵尼柄橇　陀丹衛琉　兌仁得

Purely denotative transcription: 神乃裁 = judgment of
God, *kami-no-sabaki*; 神性審判 = divine judgment, *shinsei-shinpan*; 神乃審理 = divine judgment, *kami-no-shinri*.

Phonetic & denotative transcription: 大仁慧流 = great benevolence
and wisdom flowed (to men) = hence "God has judged."

Phonetic & eulogistic transcription: 陀仁恵婁 = Buddha often
gives benevolence; 堕児壊流 = one who corrects lazy kids; 大丹
重瑠 = a large, heavy, red gem; 妥仁得 = one who compromises to
obtain benevolence.

Attention-getting transcription: 壁蝨得 = a mite catcher; 蛇児会
婁 = a kid who often meets a snake = a snake-loving kid; 蛇似兄留
= a brother who resembles a snake; 惰児廻留 = a lazy child playing.

Dave

(m) Pet form of David (LDWG); see David

Kana transcription: ディブ／でいぶ

Purely phonetic transcription: 泥部　襧位武
祢偉奉　弟威務　出畏輔　弟意負

Purely denotative transcription: See David

Phonetic & denotative transcription: 出慰務 = a one who is in
charge of consoling = hence "darling"; 弟慰舞 = a brother who
dances for consolation = hence "darling."

Phonetic & eulogistic transcription: 出意輔 = one who has the
intention of helping; 弟威武 = a brother who is a dignified samurai;
出偉豊 = one who has become great and rich.

Attention-getting transcription: 出胃部 = one whose belly
protrudes; 出猪舞 = a badger which has come out to dance.

Brainteaser: 日霧 = a fog in the daytime. Note: "Da-" (= day) = 日 in
Japanese. Hence it is read "Dave."

David

(m) Hebrew, originally a lullaby word meaning "darling", then "friend" (EGW)

可憐

Kana transcription: デイヴィッド／でぃびぃっど

Purely phonetic transcription: 泥備度　襧美土
祢日努　瀰媚弩　瀰毘導　弟比怒　出琵奴

Purely denotative transcription: 可憐 = lovable, darling, *karen*; 愛人 = a sweetheart, lover, *aijin*; 恋人 = a sweetheart, lover, *koibito*; 情人 = a sweetheart, lover, *jojin*; 友達 = a friend, *tomodachi*.

Phonetic & denotative transcription: 出美奴 = a good-looking fellow = hence "darling"; 弟魅努 = a brother trying to be handsome = hence "darling."

Phonetic & eulogistic transcription: 出美童 = an outstandingly handsome child; 弟避怒 = a brother who avoids anger; 出非度 = one who climbs to unusual heights in social success.

Attention-getting transcription: 出鼻怒 = one with an angrily protruding nose; 出肥度 = one who is outstandingly fat.

Deborah

(f) A Hebrew, "a bee" later, "eloquent" or "oracle" (HS)

雄弁

Kana transcription: デボラ／でぼら

Purely phonetic transcription: 出母等　弟模羅
出菩驟　出慕鑼　出簿喇　出莫良　弟暮蘿

Purely denotative transcription: 蜂 = a bee, *hachi* and 雄弁 = eloquent, *yuben*; 哲人 = a philosopher, *tetsujin*; 賢人 = a wise man, *kenjin*.

Phonetic & denotative transcription: 出忙等 = those which go out in a busy way = a "bee"; 泥房等 = those in the mud cells = "bees."

Phonetic & eulogistic transcription: 出望喇 = a trumpet which brings hope; 出貌良 = one who has outstandingly good looks; 弟防良 = one who defends his younger brother well.

Attention-getting transcription: 出肪良 = one who is quite fat; 出暴驟 = a mule that turns violent; 出姥裸 = an old woman who goes out in the nude.

Denise

(F) Feminine form of Dennis (LDWG); see Dennis

Kana transcription: デニーズ／でにーず

Purely phonetic transcription: 出弐位頭　出荷威逗 弟仁偉徒　弟丹豆　出尼杜

Purely denotative transcription: See Dennis

Phonetic & denotative transcription: 酊仁慰頭 = a drunk, benevolent and consoling boss = "goddess of wine."

Phonetic & eulogistic transcription: 出仁偉頭 = a great benevolent boss; 出新医徒 = a new medical student; 出任移豆 = one who is in charge of shipping beans; 出忍医頭 = a tolerant boss of doctors; 出認違図 = one who accepts a different plan; 出児医途 = a pediatrician on his way (for consultation).

Attention-getting transcription: 出丹猪杜 = a red wild boar which has come out of the forest; 出妊威頭 = a dignified boss who has become pregnant.

Dennis

(m) Greek, from Dionysus, "god of wine" (ECS)

Kana transcription: デニス／でにす

Purely phonetic transcription: 出弐巣　出荷州 弟仁諏　弟丹須　出尼数

Purely denotative transcription: 酒神 = a god of wine, *sakagami* or *shushin*.

Phonetic & denotative transcription: 出荷酒 = one who consigns wine = hence "god of wine"; 出任酒 = one in charge of wine = hence "god of wine"; 出入酒 = a wine steward = hence "god of wine."

Phonetic & eulogistic transcription: 出仁主 = a benevolent master; 出新子 = a newborn child; 出荷首 = a shipping manager; 出忍司 = a tolerant official; 出刃守 = a sword keeper.

Attention-getting transcription: 出妊司 = an official who makes (women) pregnant; 出児守 = a babysitter who makes housecalls.

Brainteaser: 日荷主 = a manager in charge of a day's burden. Note: "De-" (= day) = 日 in Japanese. Hence it is read "Dennis."

Derek
(m) British form of Theodore (LDWG); see Theodore

Kana transcription: ドレック／どれっく

Purely phonetic transcription: 努霊駆　瞳麗究　導礼公　道嶺宮　藤苔供

Purely denotative transcription: See Theodore

Phonetic & denotative transcription: 統励公 = to try to rule the public = hence "people, ruler."

Phonetic & eulogistic transcription: 努礼究 = one who seeks courtesy; 能怜公 = an able wise duke; 度励苦 = one who often attempts painful undertakings; 導礼供 = one who leads and offers courtesy.

Attention-getting transcription: 怒霊苦 = an angry ghost with pain; 童怜狗 = a clever puppy.

Diana
(f) Greek, "goddess of the moon, of hunting and of virginity" (WNWD)

Kana transcription: ダイアナ／だいあな

Purely phonetic transcription: 打異阿菜　駄位亜名　陀伊婀奈　舵偉雅娜　第孔　大亜那　代鴉南　台穴

Purely denotative transcription: 月神 = the goddess of the moon, *gesshin*; 狩猟神 = the goddess of hunting, *shuryoshin*;　純潔神 = the goddess of virginity, *jun-ketsushin*; 処女神 = the goddess of virginity, *shojogami*.

Phonetic & denotative transcription: 舵食雅娜 = a beauty who controls the beautiful eclipse = hence "the goddess of the moon"; 拿以穴 = one who catches by means of a pitfall = hence "the goddess of hunting"; 打猪穴 = one who hits a wild boar in a pitfall = hence "the goddess of hunting."

Phonetic & eulogistic transcription: 大雅娜名 = a very famous elegant beauty; 大雅那 = extremely elegant and beautiful; 題雅名 = much talked about famous elegance.

Attention-getting transcription: 惰猪雅南 = a lazy, but elegant wild boar in the south; 大蛙名 = a famous big frog.

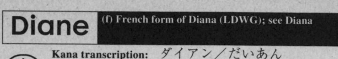

Diane

(f) French form of Diana (LDWG); see Diana

Kana transcription: ダイアン／だいあん

Purely phonetic transcription: 大安　耐行　醍杏
提案　題按　内鞍　代庵

Purely denotative transcription: See Diana

Phonetic & denotative transcription: 舵食暗 = one who controls the eclipse to cause darkness = hence "the goddess of the moon"; 拿猪暗 = one who catches a wild boar in the dark = hence " the goddess of hunting"; 打猪鞍 = one who hits a wild boar from the saddle = hence "the goddess of hunting."

Phonetic & eulogistic transcription: 娜偉安 = a peaceful great beauty; 娜雅鞍 = an elegant beauty in the saddle; 娜威庵 = a dignified beauty at her vacation home.

Attention-getting transcription: 娜猪雅運 = a beautiful woman who carries a wild boar; 惰猪雅雲 = a lazy wild boar under an elegant cloud; 蛇威闇 = a horrifying snake in the dark; 大蛙運 = a lucky big frog.

Brainteaser: 染行 = one who dyes; 染雅雲 = a cloud dyed elegantly. Note: "Di-" (dye) = 染 in Japanese. Hence it is read "Diane."

Dick

(m) Rhyming pet name of Richard (LDWG); see Richard

Kana transcription: デック／でっく

Purely phonetic transcription: 出供　出宮　弟公
弟究　出駆　弟功　出玖

Purely denotative transcription: See Richard

Phonetic & denotative transcription: 出威宮 = a dignitary who comes out of the palace = hence "ruler, hard."

Phonetic & eulogistic transcription: 出宮 = one who comes out of the palace = hence a noble person; 弟公 = a younger brother who is a duke; 弟究 = a studious younger brother; 弟功 = a younger brother with merits; 出玖 = a gem which has come out (of the earth).

Attention-getting transcription: 弟駈 = a running younger brother; 出狗 = a dog which came out; 弟苦 = a younger brother in trouble.

Dinah

(f) Hebrew, "judged, vindicated"; Biblical, the daughter of Leah and Jacob (LDWG)

Kana transcription: ダイナ／だいな

Purely phonetic transcription: 舵位名　陀異菜
駄偉那　打意娜　妥委奈　大菜

Purely denotative transcription: 審判 = judgment, *shinpan*; 判定 = judgment, *hantei*; 立証 = vindication, *rissho*.

Phonetic & denotative transcription: 大意納 = great opinion given = hence "judged, vindicated."

Phonetic & eulogistic transcription: 大名 = great fame or feudal lord; 大医娜 ; a great female doctor; 大位娜 = a high-ranking beautiful lady.

Attention-getting transcription: 惰威那 = lazy, dignified and beautiful; 醍名 = a famous wine; 大娜 = a beautiful tall girl.

Donald

(m) Celtic, "world" and "mighty" (EGW)

努
成
度

Kana transcription: ドナルド／どなるど

Purely phonetic transcription: 土菜瑠土　度名琉奴
怒奈榁動　努成度　呶鳴弩

Purely denotative transcription: 世界的力 = world-level strength, *sekaiteki chikara*; 世界勢力 = world power, *sekai seiryoku*; 世界一大力 = the greatest power in the world, *sekaiichi tairiki*; 天下一力持 = the world's most powerful man, *rikiji*.

Phonetic & denotative transcription: 努難流導 = overcoming difficulty with ease = hence "mighty"; 怒難漏呶 = to shout angrily to drive away difficulties = hence "mighty."

Phonetic & eulogistic transcription: 導難流度 = one who often leads the way in solving problems; 能納留怒 = one who can calm anger; 働成道 = one who builds a road.

Attention-getting transcription: 怒名留洞 = an angrily named cave; 童鳴怒 = an angry boy who is shouting.

Donna
(f) Italian, Latin, "lady" (LDWG)

Kana transcription: ドナ／どな

Purely phonetic transcription: 丼名　曇菜　鈍奈
罎娜　遁那　呑南 or 努菜　度名　土菜　弩那
呶娜　導南　努奈　怒納

Purely denotative transcription: 貴婦人 = a lady, *kifujin*; 淑女 = a lady, *shukujo*; 婦人 = a woman, *fujin*; 女 = a woman, *onna*; 女性 = a woman, *josei*; 婦女 = a woman, *fujo*.

Phonetic & denotative transcription: 土娜 = a local beauty = hence a "lady"; 努娜 = a diligent beauty = hence a "lady"; 働娜 = a working beauty = hence a "lady."

Phonetic & eulogistic transcription: 敦娜 = a sincere beauty; 嫩娜 = a cute lady; 努那 = diligent and beautiful; 脳娜 = an intelligent beauty.

Attention-getting transcription: 鈍娜 = a dull beauty; 怒娜 = an angry beauty; 呶娜 = a noisy beauty.

Doreen
(f) Pet form of Dorothy (RGS); see Dorothy

Kana transcription: ドリーン／どりーん

Purely phonetic transcription: 努利院　度麗姻
脳吏引　憧李音　導離員

Purely denotative transcription: See Dorothy

Phonetic & denotative transcription: 能霊引 = abilities granted one by a spirit = hence "gift of God";
導霊姻 = a marriage guided by the spirit = "gift of God."

Phonetic & eulogistic transcription: 努怜引 = one who strives to be clever; 導麗姻 = a successful matchmaker; 度励員 = one who frequently makes efforts.

Attention-getting transcription: 怒霊胤 = a descendant of an angry ghost; 童嶺隠 = a child who hides on the ridge; 脳零員 = one who has no brain at all; 怒鈴音 = a bell which makes angry sounds.

Doris

(f) Greek, a region of central Greece (LDWG)

Kana transcription: ドリス／どりす

Purely phonetic transcription: 土理州　努離巣
度里数　怒麗須　能俐諏　呹利寿　奴履司

Purely denotative transcription: 中央希臘婦人 = a lady of central Greece, *chuo girisha fujin*; 中央希臘女 = a woman of central Greece, *girsha onna*; 希臘女性 = a Greek woman, *girisha josei*.

Phonetic & denotative transcription: 渡臘子 = a woman who came from Greece = hence a "woman from Doris."

Phonetic & eulogistic transcription: 努利子 = a diligent and clever girl; 敦麗子 = a sincere and elegant girl; 嫩理子 = a cute and wise lady; 努麗子 = a diligent and beautiful girl.

Attention-getting transcription: 怒麗子 = an angry elegant girl; 祷霊守 = a fortune teller; 呹狸子 = a noisy baby badger.

Dorothy

(f) Latin, Greek, "gift of God" (WNWD)

土路詞

Kana transcription: ドロシー／どろしー

Purely phonetic transcription: 土路詞　度炉士
弩侶詩　呹慮志　藤露資　怒呂至　努旅史

Purely denotative transcription: 神乃進物 = a gift of God, *kami-no-shinmotsu*; 神乃贈答品 = a gift of God, *kami-no-zotohin*; 神乃恵物 = a God's gift, *kami-no-keibutsu*; 神乃贈遺 = a God's gift, *kami-no-zoi*.

Phonetic & denotative transcription: 導良神意 = The will of God which guides man to good = hence "gift of God"; 動露神威 = the dignity of God which appears = hence "gift of God."

Phonetic & eulogistic transcription: 憧虜神偉 = one who longs to become a slave of God's greatness; 働良示畏 = one who works hard to show respect; 能露姉偉 = a great sister with capacities.

Attention-getting transcription: 泥獅威 = a dignified lioness which is muddy; 洞狼示威 = a wolf in the cave showing dignity.

Douglas

(m) Gaelic, "dark blue" (EGW)

 濃青

Kana transcription: ダグラス／だぐらす

Purely phonetic transcription: 妥具等州　打倶蘿酸　駄虞喇簾　陀寓良司　舵遇喇寿　柁愚良諏

Purely denotative transcription: 濃青 = dark blue, *no-sei*; 濃青色 = dark blue color, *no-sei-shoku*; 深青 = dark blue, *shin-sei*; 深碧 = dark blue color, *shin-heki*.

Phonetic & denotative transcription: 藤具羅周 = a thin cloth around the wisteria (= blue) = hence "dark blue."

Phonetic & eulogistic transcription: 導求良素 = one who seeks to be good and honest; 童求螺巣 = a child who looks for snail nests; 陀救良子 = a Buddha who saves naked children; 大求良主 = a great master who seeks to be good.

Attention-getting transcription: 蛇求螺子 = a snake which seeks young snails; 打球良司 = an official who hits balls well.

Duncan

(m) Celtic name, Modern Gaelic, "brown warrior" (LDWG)

男敢

Kana transcription: ダンカン／だんかん

Purely phonetic transcription: 断観　談冠　段幹　壇間　団感　弾官　男敢　暖巻　但関

Purely denotative transcription: 茶戦士 = a brown warrior, *chasenshi*; 茶色武人 = a brown warrior, *chairo bujin*; 茶頭武士 = a brown-headed warrior, *chato bushi*.

Phonetic & denotative transcription: 男敢 = a brave man = hence "warrior"; 断官 = an officer whose decisions are excellent = hence "warrior"; 団幹 = a chief officer of the troop = hence "warrior."

Phonetic & eulogistic transcription: 談官 = a spokesman; 暖寛 = warm and generous; 男監 = a male administrator; 檀冠 = a crown made of the rose of Sharon; 男神 = a male god.

Attention-getting transcription: 弾棺 = ammunition in coffins = hence peace; 断閑 = one who cuts his leisure time.

Eddie
(m) Pet form of Edward, Edgar (LDWG); see Edward, Edgar

Kana transcription: エデイ／えでい

Purely phonetic transcription: 江出意　恵弟偉　慧出威　衛弟畏　重出位　兄祢

Purely denotative transcription: See Edward

Phonetic & denotative transcription: 栄出偉 = one who is prosperous and great = hence "rich"; 衛弟威 = a dignified younger brother who guards = hence "guardian."

Phonetic & eulogistic transcription: 衛出威 = one who comes to protect with dignity; 恵出慰 = one who spreads benevolence and consolation; 慧弟偉 = a great wise younger brother; 英出医 = a doctor who comes from England.

Attention-getting transcription: 泳出猪 = a swimming wild boar; 会弟猪 = a younger brother who meets a wild boar.

Edgar
(m) Old English, compound of "rich" and "spear" (GRS)

Kana transcription: エドガー／えどがー

Purely phonetic transcription: 柄度画雅　絵土我亜　江努賀阿　依怒雅　柄度画　絵土我　江努賀　恵道牙　江戸鷲　餌奴伽　会孥苛

Purely denotative transcription: 富槍 = rich and spear, *fuso*; 富裕槍 = rich and spear, *fuyu so*; 裕福鎗 = rich and spear, *yufuku so*.

Phonetic & denotative transcription: 柄導牙 = a shaft which leads to a tusk = hence a "spear"; 栄度芽雅 = prosperity blooming beautifully = hence "rich."

Phonetic & eulogistic transcription: 重度賀雅 = one who makes great festivities very often; 恵渡我雅 = I bring elegance and benevolence; 慧努芽 = one who endeavors to engender wisdom; 栄土河 = a river in the rich land.

Attention-getting transcription: 重怒鷲 = a goose whose anger is doubled; 江戸画 = a picture from Edo; 江戸蛾 = a type of moth found in Edo.

61

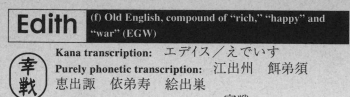

Edith

(f) Old English, compound of "rich," "happy" and "war" (EGW)

Kana transcription: エデイス／えでいす

Purely phonetic transcription: 江出州　餌弟須　恵出諏　依弟寿　絵出巣

Purely denotative transcription: 富戦 = rich and war, *fusen*; 幸戦 = happy and war, *kosen*; 幸福戦争 = happy and war, *kofukusen*; 富裕戦争 = rich and war, *fuyusen*.

Phonetic & denotative transcription: 会泥子 = to see muddy children = hence a "war"; 壊出州 = to break down a country = hence a "war"; 栄出州 = a prosperous state = hence "rich."

Phonetic & eulogistic transcription: 慧出偉子 = a wise great child; 恵出異主 = an unusually benevolent master; 画出司 = an official who appears in the picture; 重出寿 = one who enjoys doubled longevity; 会出寿 = one who offers longevity.

Attention-getting transcription: 潰出司 = a governor who suffers from an ulcer; 泳出雛 = a swimming fledgling.

Edward

(m) Old English, "rich guardian" (ECS)

Kana transcription: エドワード／えどわーど

Purely phonetic transcription: 絵土和阿土　絵土和土　柄啾輪啾　餌努倭努　画度琶度　衛童環度

Purely denotative transcription: 富裕保護者 = rich guardian, *fuyu hogosha*; 裕福守護 = rich guardian, *yufuku shugo*; 金持後見人 = rich guardian, *kanemochi kokennin*.

Phonetic & denotative transcription: 衛努話雅度 = one who often negotiates smartly trying to guard = hence a "guardian."

Phonetic & eulogistic transcription: 慧奴和雅度 = an intelligent fellow who often makes smart agreements; 重度話努 = one who tries to make frequent negotiations.

Attention-getting transcription: 兄動和蛙怒 = an elder brother who is angry with the Japanese frogs moving around.

Edwin
(m) Old English, compound of "happy"; "rich"; and "friend" (EGW)

Kana transcription: エドウイン／えどういん

Purely phonetic transcription: 絵度右韻　餌土鵜院　柄怒右印　恵働優引　衛努憂員　画啄雨韻

Purely denotative transcription: 幸友 = a happy friend, *koyu*; 幸福友人 = a happy friend, *kofuku yujin*; 幸運友生 = a happy friend, *koun yusei*.

Phonetic & denotative transcription: 栄努優員 = a rich, diligent, kind person = hence "happy, rich" and "friend."

Phonetic & eulogistic transcription: 慧童有隠 = a child who has hidden intelligence; 兄導優引 = a brother who brings tenderness.

Attention-getting transcription: 江渡鵜蔭 = the shadow of a cormorant flying over the bay; 恵度鵜姻 = a cormorant which is lucky enough to marry often.

Elaine
(f) Greek "light"; "bright one" (ECS)

Kana transcription: エレイン／えれいん

Purely phonetic transcription: 絵例員　柄冷院　江霊印　餌玲因　衛令引　画礼飲　恵麗隠

Purely denotative transcription: 光 = light, *hikari*; 光輝 = brightness, *koki*; 晃耀 = brightness, *koyo*; 光晃 = brightness, *koko* or 秀才 = bright one, *shusai*.

Phonetic & denotative transcription: 慧藜員 = one whose wisdom is bright = hence "light, bright one"; 重伶引 = one who helps direct wisdom = hence "light, bright one"; 会聆因 = one who introduces wisdom = hence "light, bright one"; 兄怜隠 = an elder brother with hidden wisdom = hence "light, bright one."

Phonetic & eulogistic transcription: 重麗姻 = a very graceful marriage; 慧怜音 = one who sounds intelligent and wise; 重聆胤 = a descendant who inherits wisdom.

Attention-getting transcription: 絵隷引 = a slave charmed by pictures = a picture lover; 永霊院 = an eternal ghost in the temple.

Eleanor
(f) A form of Helen (EGW); see Helen

英明麗人

Kana transcription: エレアノール／えれあのーる

Purely phonetic transcription: 絵例雅野緒留
英冷阿脳妻　叡霊亜能瑠　栄玲唖濃漏

Purely denotative transcription: See Helen

Phonetic & denotative transcription: 映励雅脳留 = one who improves her brain to be bright and elegant = hence "bright one, shining one"; 英怜雅能留 = one who is bright, wise, elegant and capable = hence "bright one, shining one."

Phonetic & eulogistic transcription: 慧怜雅濃留 = one whose wisdom and elegance are thick (outstanding); 叡礼雅納留 = one who is endowed with wisdom, courtesy and elegance; 鋭伶雅脳留 = one who has a sharp elegant brain.

Attention-getting transcription: 慧零雅悩蛙 = an elegant frog in trouble which has no wisdom at all; 泳麗婀農留 = an elegant and beautiful swimming female farmer.

Elizabeth
(f) Hebrew, "God hath sworn" or "oath of God" (HS)

神乃約束

Kana transcription: エリザベス／えりざべす

Purely phonetic transcription: 襟座部州　衿坐琶諏
江利座部州　絵理坐辺巣　慧里座琶寿

Purely denotative transcription: 神乃約束 = oath of God, *kami-no-yakusoku*; 神乃宣誓 = oath of God, *kami-no-sensei*.

Phonetic & denotative transcription: 恵霊座辺蘇 = the benevolence of the spirit which revives around us = hence "oath of God"; 叡理座迷守 = providence which guards the delusion lying around us = hence "oath of God."

Phonetic & eulogistic transcription: 永理座辺守 = truth which will guard us eternally; 恵理座部子 = a benevolent and wise village child; 慧霊座部周 = a spirit of wisdom living around the village.

Attention-getting transcription: 鋭狸座部巣 = a smart badger in the nest; 泳鯉座辺洲 = a carp swimming around the sand bank.

Ellen

(f) English form of Helen (LDWG); see Helen

Kana transcription: エレン／えれん

Purely phonetic transcription: 絵例園　重冷艶
江霊羨 and also 恵練　衛蓮　画恋　慧漣　叡連

Purely denotative transcription:　See Helen

Phonetic & denotative transcription:　映練 = one who practices to be bright = hence "bright one, shining one"; 英憐 = one who is bright and lovable = hence "bright one, shining one."

Phonetic & eulogistic transcription:　慧憐 = one who is wise and lovable; 叡練 = one who trains herself to be intelligent; 鋭恋 = a sharp love; 英蓮 = an English lotus; 永蓮 = an eternal lotus.

Attention-getting transcription:　影恋 = a love in the shadows; 江漣 = mild waves in the inlet; 泳蓮 = a swimming lotus.

Elliot

(m) Surname used as a first name, originally in Scotland, which means "high" (EGW)

Kana transcription: エリオット／えりおっと

Purely phonetic transcription: 江利尾都　絵理緒戸
慧里御徒　恵李雄途　画履夫　柄離於妬　襟夫

Purely denotative transcription: 高位 = a high rank, *koi*; 上位 = an upper rank, *joi*; 高隆 = high, *koryu*; 沖天 = high, *chuten*; 長身 = high stature, *choshin*; 高峻 = high (mountain), *koshun*.

Phonetic & denotative transcription: 慧理雄登 = an intelligent hero who goes high = hence "high"; 慧利王塔 = a clever king's tower = hence "high"; 栄利圧騰 = increasing profits = "high."

Phonetic & eulogistic transcription: 栄吏夫 = a husband who is a prosperous official; 恵利夫 = a benevolent and clever husband; 慧理夫 = an intelligent husband; 鋭利夫 = an extremely clever husband; 慧利雄頭 = a clever heroic chief.

Attention-getting transcription: 衣離夫 = a husband who takes off his clothes; 壊理悪頭 = a bad chief who loses his temper; 餌離烏妬 = a jealous crow who is far from the feed; 栄離夫 = a husband who has passed his prime age (= prosperity).

Emily (f) Latin-Germanic, "affable"; "worker" (ECS)

Kana transcription: エミリー／えみりー

Purely phonetic transcription: 江未里委　絵実理意
江未里　絵実理　慧魅里　恵身李　画美履位

Purely denotative transcription: 愛敬 = affable, *aikyo*; 愛
想 = affable, *aikyo* or 労働者 = a worker, *rodosha*.

Phonetic & denotative transcription: 恵魅利威 = benevolent,
charming, clever and dignified = hence "affable"; 笑麗 = an elegant
smile = hence "affable"; 英御霊 = a respectful bright spirit = hence
"affable"; 重魅礼 = doubled charm and courtesy = hence "affable";
永魅礼 = eternal charm and courtesy = hence "affable.

Phonetic & eulogistic transcription: 慧魅麗医 = a wise, charming
and elegant doctor; 絵美麗 = one who is as beautiful as a picture;
永美麗 = one who is eternally beautiful and elegant.

Attention-getting transcription: 壊魅礼 = one who destroys charm
and courtesy; 泳御霊 = a swimming ghost.

Emma (f) Old German, "whole"; "universal" (EGW)

Kana transcription: エマ／えま

Purely phonetic transcription: 絵間　江魔　画真
恵馬　慧摩　衛麻

Purely denotative transcription: 全体 = whole, *zentai*; 全
部 = whole, *zenbu*; 統一 = universal, *toitsu*; 普遍 = universal,
uhen; 全般 = universal, *zenpan*.

Phonetic & denotative transcription: 永真 = eternal truth = hence
"whole, universal."

Phonetic & eulogistic transcription: 重真 = truth doubled; 衛真 =
one who defends the truth; 慧磨 = one who improves intelligence;
慧馬 = a wise horse; 叡真 = intelligence and truth.

Attention-getting transcription: 恵魔 = a benevolent demon; 慧魔 =
a wise demon; 宴馬 = a feasting horse; 宴魔 = a feasting demon.

66

Eric
(m) Old Norse, "ever king" (ECS)

Kana transcription: エリック／えりっく

Purely phonetic transcription: 異離句　位里苦
医理宮　委麗久　伊利玖　偉梨究　威裏倶

Purely denotative transcription: 永遠王 = an eternal king, *eien o*; 永久王 = an eternal king, *eikyu o*; 不朽王 = an ever king, *fukyu o*.

Phonetic & denotative transcription: 永齢宮 = an eternal palace = "ever king"; 永令功 = an eternal meritorious deed = "ever king."

Phonetic & eulogistic transcription: 恵理久 = one who has eternal benevolence and wisdom; 慧理究 = one who seeks wisdom and intelligence; 兄悧駆 = an elder brother who makes use of cleverness; 栄利久 = one who has eternal prosperity.

Attention-getting transcription: 慧狸駈 = a clever badger which is running; 泳浬狗 = a dog swimming nautical miles; 英吏苦 = a bright official who is troubled; 鋭狸吼 = a badger shouting (roaring) sharply.

Erica
(f) Feminine form of Eric (LDWG); see Eric

Kana transcription: エリカ／えりか

Purely phonetic transcription: 異離香　位里華
医理歌　委麗霞　伊利嫁　偉梨賀　威裏佳

Purely denotative transcription: See Eric

Phonetic & denotative transcription: 永齢華 = an eternal splendor = hence an "ever king/queen"; 永令花 = an eternal flower = hence an "ever king/queen."

Phonetic & eulogistic transcription: 恵理花 = a benevolent and wise flower; 慧理誇 = one who is proud of wisdom and intelligence; 永悧華 = cleverness and splendor; 栄利嫁 = a prosperous clever bride; 盈利家 = a house filled with a fortune.

Attention-getting transcription: 慧狸嫁 = a clever badger's bride; 泳浬鹿 = a deer swimming nautical miles; 英吏暇 = a bright official who has nothing to do; 会狸嘩 = a noisy badger's meeting.

Ernest

(m) Old German, "vigor"; "earnestness" (EGW)

真卒

Kana transcription: アーネスト／あーねすと

Purely phonetic transcription: 亜雅値洲渡　雅値洲渡　阿根諏徒　雅音寿途　蛙襧巣戸

Purely denotative transcription: 活力 = vigor, *katsuryoku*; 精力 = vigor, *seiryoku*; 活気 = vigor, *katsuryoku* or 真直 = earnestness, *shojiki*; 堅気 = earnestness, *katagi*; 真面目 = earnestness, *majime*; 真剣 = earnestness, *shinken*.

Phonetic & denotative transcription: 闘根酔途 = to nip foolishness in the bud = hence to be "earnest, sober"; 雅寧素度 = often elegant, polite and honest = hence "earnestness."

Phonetic & eulogistic transcription: 雅寧守杜 = an elegant and polite forest guard; 雅嶺守頭 = the guard chief of the elegant ridge; 雅音素頭 = an honest chief who speaks elegantly.

Attention-getting transcription: 蛙音洲渡 = a frog which cries on the sand banks; 鴉子巣途 = a baby crow on its way to its nest.

Brainteaser: 鴉巣 = a crow's nest; 雅巣 = an elegant nest. Note: "-nest" = 巣 in Japanese. Hence both are read "Ernest."

Ernie

(m) Pet form of Ernest (LDWG); see Ernest

Kana transcription: アーニー／あーにー

Purely phonetic transcription: 亜雅児位　阿亜荷偉　雅阿丹威 and also 雅迩　阿荷　雅児

Purely denotative transcription: See Ernest

Phonetic & denotative transcription: 雅唖仁意 = one who smiles elegantly and has a benevolent intention = "earnest"; 雅仁畏 = one who is elegant, benevolent and respected = "earnestness."

Phonetic & eulogistic transcription: 唖雅児偉 = a great child who laughs elegantly; 雅仁医 = an elegant and benevolent doctor; 雅児威 = an elegant and dignified child.

Attention-getting transcription: 蛙唖耳異 = a laughing frog who has strange ears; 鴉児医 = a doctor who treats young crows.

Eugine (m) Greek, "wellborn"; "noble" (ECS)

Kana transcription: ユウジン／ゆうじん

Purely phonetic transcription: 友人　夕神　優仁
憂陣　右臣　有靭　結刃　勇迅　佑侭　悠尽

Purely denotative transcription: 良家子女 = wellborn, *ryoke shijo*; 名門出 = wellborn, *meimonde*; 名家生 = wellborn, *meika umare* or 高貴 = noble, *koki*; 貴戚 = noble, *kiseki*; 貴尊 = noble, *kison*; 貴人 = a noble person, *kijin*.

Phonetic & denotative transcription: 遊人 = a playboy = "wellborn"; 裕人 = an well-off person = "wellborn"; 悠人 = an well-off person = "wellborn"; 優仁 = tender and benevolent = "wellborn."

Phonetic & eulogistic transcription: 雄人 = a heroic person; 勇人 = a courageous person; 友人 = a friend; 佑神 = divine help.

Attention-getting transcription: 油人 = an oil businessman; 熊迅 = a swift bear; 憂人 = a melancholy person; 熊神 = a divine bear.

Eve (f) Hebrew, "life," for the first Eve was "the mother of all living" (HS)

Kana transcription: イーヴ／いーヴ

Purely phonetic transcription: 位位部　偉位歩
畏依不　伊医負　委委蒲　衣胃撫　尉以武

Purely denotative transcription: 生命 = life, *seimei*; 命 = life, *inochi*; 命脈 = life, *meimyaku*; 身命 = life, *shinmyo*; 生気 = life, *seiki*.

Phonetic & denotative transcription: 衣食捕 = to obtain clothing and food = the mother of all living = hence "life"; 囲食豊 = rich food around us = the mother of all living = hence "life"; 施食豊 = to provide abundant food = hence "life."

Phonetic & eulogistic transcription: 威偉舞 = a great dignified dancer; 異偉務 = an unusually great position; 施衣豊 = one richly dressed; 威猪捕 = a great boar hunter.

Attention-getting transcription: 葦移鵡 = a parrot moving among the reeds; 囲猪霧 = a boar surrounded by the fog.

Evelyn
(f) Celtic-Latin, "pleasant"; "life"; "hazel" (HS)

Kana transcription: イヴリン／いゔりん

Purely phonetic transcription: 位部林　威分輪
偉歩燐　畏不倫　意符厘　伊負臨　委蒲隣

Purely denotative transcription: 生命 = life, *seimei*; 命 = life, *inochi*; 生気 = life, *seiki*; 命脈 = life, *meimyaku*; 身命 = life, *shinmyo* or 榛 = hazel, *hashibami*.

Phonetic & denotative transcription: 食捕林 = to obtain food in the woods = hence "life"; 食豊隣 = rich food near us = hence "life."

Phonetic & eulogistic transcription: 偉舞練 = a great dance instructor; 偉務麗員 = an elegant dancer; 衣豊伶院 = a richly dressed beautiful ex-empress; 畏奉鈴 = a respectfully offered bell.

Attention-getting transcription: 猪舞林 = a boar dancing in the woods; 移鵡林 = a parrot moving in the forest; 猪撫麗員 = a beautiful boar tamer.

Florence
(m) Latin, "flower"; "flourishing"; "of Florence" (ECS)

Kana transcription: フローレンス／ふろーれんす

Purely phonetic transcription: 富浪連洲　不労練寿
府朗恋巣　豊老憐須　付滝廉簾　賦牢煉素

Purely denotative transcription: 花 = a flower, *hana*; 華 = a flower, *hana*; 花盛 = flourishing, *hanazakari*; 満開 = full bloom, *mankai*; 開花 = bloom, *kaika*.

Phonetic & denotative transcription: 豊良蓮蘇 = a revived lotus that is rich and good = hence "flourishing"; 不老蓮寿 = a long-living lotus which does not get old = hence "flourishing."

Phonetic & eulogistic transcription: 豊労練主 = a master who works hard to get rich; 不老恋手 = a lovemaking expert who never gets old; 扶老憐子 = a child who likes and cares for elderly people.

Attention-getting transcription: 撫弄恋手 = a lovemaking expert with good hands; 不労恋手 = a jobless playboy; 婦弄恋手 = a lovemaking expert who plays with ladies.

Frances (f) The feminine form of Francis (LDWG); see Francis

Kana transcription: フランセス／ふらんせす

Purely phonetic transcription: 府欄世洲　富覧瀬須　父蘭施巣　賦卵勢諏　豊嵐背寿　布乱盛簾

Purely denotative transcription: See Francis

Phonetic & denotative transcription: 仏蘭西子 = a child of France = hence "Frenchman/Frenchwoman."

Phonetic & eulogistic transcription: 仏蘭世守 = one who guards French society = hence "Jeannne d'Arc"; 豊卵生巣 = a rich egg laid in the nest; 不乱妻寿 = an chaste long-living wife; 負乱勢諏 = one who defeats a rebellion by persuasion; 負濫勢司 = one who defeats a rotten powerful official; 婦蘭生蘇 = a woman who restores an orchid.

Attention-getting transcription: 怖嵐施守 = a guardian who makes a fearful storm; 撫乱妻子 = one who consoles a mad wife and children; 怖乱妻主 = a fearful mad hostess.

Francis (m) Latin, "a Frenchman," formerly "Frank" (LDWG)

Kana transcription: フランシス／ふらんしす

Purely phonetic transcription: 府欄市洲　富覧詩須　父蘭師巣　賦卵氏諏　豊嵐誌寿　布乱紙簾

Purely denotative transcription: 仏蘭西人 = a Frenchman, *furansu-jin*; 仏国人 = a Frenchman, *futsukoku-jin*.

Phonetic & denotative transcription: 仏蘭西子 = a child of France = hence "Frenchman."

Phonetic & eulogistic transcription: 富蘭姿守 = a guardian in the shape of an rich orchid; 豊卵飼巣 = a rich egg in the nest; 不乱士主 = an unshaken samurai chief; 負乱獅主 = a boss who defeats a rampant lion; 負濫守司 = one who defeats a rotten governor; 夫蘭死蘇 = a husband who restores a dead orchid.

Attention-getting transcription: 怖嵐姿守 = a guardian in the shape of a fearful storm; 撫乱獅子 = one who tames a rampant young lion; 撫乱髭主 = a master who touches disorderly beards.

71

Frank
(m) Pet form of Francis (LDWG); see Francis

Kana transcription: フランク／ふらんく

Purely phonetic transcription: 府欄久　富覧供
父蘭救　賦卵究　豊嵐玖　布乱駆　符濫宮

Purely denotative transcription: See Francis

Phonetic & denotative transcription: 仏蘭公 = a French duke = hence "Frenchman."

Phonetic & eulogistic transcription: 富蘭供 = one who supplies rich orchids = hence an orchid grower; 仏蘭救 = one who saves France; 不乱公 = an unshaken duke; 負乱駒 = one who defeats a rampant horse; 負濫公 = one who defeats a rotten duke; 夫蘭究 = a husband who studies orchids.

Attention-getting transcription: 怖嵐駆 = one who controls a fearful storm; 撫乱駒 = one who tames a rampant horse = a horse tamer; 夫乱苦 = a husband who suffers terribly from pain; 豊卵鳩 = a pigeon which lays abundant eggs.

Franklin
(m) Germanic, "freeman" or "freeholder" (ECS)

Kana transcription: フランクリン／ふらんくりん

Purely phonetic transcription: 府欄苦隣　富覧究鈴
父蘭玖鱗　賦卵久倫　豊嵐宮厘　布乱句輪

Purely denotative transcription: 自由人 = a free man, *jiyujin*; 自由市民 = a free citizen, *jiyu shimin*.

Phonetic & denotative transcription: 不籃苦淋 = one who need not be imprisoned to be tortured and lonely = hence "freeman or freeholder"; 不乱苦臨 = one who need not be disturbed and suffer from pains = hence "freeman or freeholder."

Phonetic & eulogistic transcription: 豊蘭究林 = one who studies rich lotuses in the forest; 負乱救倫 = one who defeats a riot to save order; 扶蘭救林 = one who goes to the forest to save orchids.

Attention-getting transcription: 怖籃狗淋 = a fearful lonely caged dog; 歩嵐鳩林 = a pigeon walking in the forest on a stormy day.

Fred

(m) Pet form of Frederick (LDWG); see Frederick

Kana transcription: フレッド／ふれっど

Purely phonetic transcription: 符麗度　富礼努　豊鈴怒　賦嶺士　布令導　府令動　振度　触努

Purely denotative transcription: See Frederick

Phonetic & denotative transcription: 布令努 = to work to issue laws = hence "rule"; 敷令度 = to issue laws frequently = hence "peace and rule."

Phonetic & eulogistic transcription: 富礼努 = one who tries to be rich and courteous; 扶励度 = one who often encourages and supports; 豊麗努 = one who tries to become rich and elegant; 不齢童 = a child who never gets old.

Attention-getting transcription: 歩羚士 = a land where antelopes play; 怖霊怒 = a fearful angry ghost.

Brainteaser: 膚赤 = one who has red skin; 夫赤 = a red-haired or -faced husband. Note: "-red-" = 赤 in Japanese. Hence it is read "Fred."

Frederick

(m) Germanic, compound of "peace" and "rule" (GRS)

Kana transcription: フレデリック／ふれでりっく

Purely phonetic transcription: 符麗出利句　富礼弟理駄　豊鈴出里久　賦嶺弟履玖　布令出陸

Purely denotative transcription: 平穏統治 = peace and rule, *heian tochi*; 太平政治 = peace and rule, *taihei seiji*.

Phonetic & denotative transcription: 布令出利救 = to issue laws to save the public interest = hence "rule"; 敷令定里供 = to issue laws to offer peace in the villages = hence "peace and rule."

Phonetic & eulogistic transcription: 富礼弟利供 = a rich courteous young brother who offers his profits; 扶励出吏供 = an official who does his utmost to help (people); 豊励出里功 = one who goes out of his village to obtain his fortune.

Attention-getting transcription: 歩羚出里駄 = a village where antelopes play; 怖霊出里丘 = a hill where fearful ghosts appear.

Gabriel
(m) Hebrew, "God is a strong man" or "strong man of God" (EGW); an archangel

Kana transcription: ガブリエル／がぶりえる

Purely phonetic transcription: 賀武里絵留
画分理江流　牙部李慧琉　伽舞麗恵漏

Purely denotative transcription: 神強者 = God is a strong man, *kami kyogo*; 神強豪者 = God is a strong man, *kami kyogosha*; or 天使 = archangel, *tenshi*.

Phonetic & denotative transcription: 賀舞麗叡漏 = one who dances joyfully and transmits the providence of God = hence "the archangel"; 雅武霊恵留 = an elegant warrior of divine benevolence = hence a "strong man of God."

Phonetic & eulogistic transcription: 雅豊理兄留 = an elder brother who is elegant, rich and wise; 駕武理慧流 = a mounted samurai who exudes great wisdom; 賀奉吏恵瑠 = a benevolent official who offers gems for the festivities.

Attention-getting transcription: 臥武狸得 = a lying samurai who happens to get a badger; 牙部離猪留 = a wild boar who lost his tusks; 餓武鯉得 = a hungry samurai who got a carp.

Gabrielle
(f) Feminine form of Gabriel (HS); see Gabriel

Kana transcription: ガブリエル／がぶりえる

Purely phonetic transcription: 賀武里絵留
画分理江流　牙部李慧琉　伽舞麗恵漏

Purely denotative transcription: See Gabriel

Phonetic & denotative transcription: 賀舞麗叡漏 = one who dances joyfully and transmits the providence of God = "the archangel"; 雅武霊恵留 = an elegant warrior of divine benevolence = hence a "strong man of God."

Phonetic & eulogistic transcription: 雅豊理慧留 = one who is elegant, rich, wise and intelligent; 賀婦吏恵瑠 = a female official who offers gems for the festivities.

Attention-getting transcription: 臥捕狸得 = one who caught a sleeping badger; 河捕鯉得 = one who caught a carp in the river.

Gary
(m) Old German, compound of "spear" and "rule" (EGW)

Kana transcription: ガーリー／がーりー

Purely phonetic transcription: 賀雅里医　画亜理畏　牙阿李偉　伽唖麗威　俄唖裏意　画亜吏位

Purely denotative transcription: See Gerald

Phonetic & denotative transcription: 駕雅吏威 = an elegant, dignified official who rides a horse = "spear and rule."

Phonetic & eulogistic transcription: 雅唖利医 = an elegant rich doctor who is laughing ; 駕亜吏偉 = a great Asian official who is mounted; 賀雅履医 = a doctor who holds elegant festivities.

Attention-getting transcription: 賀蛙麗 = a frog's elegant felicitation; 牙雅麗 = elegant tusks; 餓鴉霊 = a ghost of a hungry crow.

George
(m) Greek, "man of the earth, farmer" (GRS)

Kana transcription: ジョージ／じょーじ

Purely phonetic transcription: 助王治　女王児　序追治　叙欧慈　情示　嬢寺　蒸士　常時　醸持

Purely denotative transcription: 土男 = an earth-man, *tsuki otoko*; 大地人 = a man of the earth, *taichi-jin*; 耕作者 = a agriculturist, *taichi-jin*; 百姓 = a farmer, *hyakusho*; 農夫 = a farmer, *nofu*.

Phonetic & denotative transcription: 地用持 = one who owns land and makes use of it = hence a "man of the earth, farmer"; 地養蒔 = one who cultivates the land and sows = hence a "man of the earth, farmer"; 地擁治 = one who takes care of land = hence a "man of the earth, farmer"; 壌治 = one who cultivates and rules the soil = hence a "man of the earth, farmer."

Phonetic & eulogistic transcription: 治養侍 = a samurai who rules and feeds people; 値擁示 = one who protects and shows the prices = a merchant; 地要飼 = one who needs land to bring up animals; 情侍 = a kindhearted samurai; 浄慈 = pure benevolence.

Attention-getting transcription: 侍酔示 = a drunken samurai; 治羊児 = a child who controls sheep; 情事 = a love affair.

Georgia

f) Feminine form of George (LDWG); see George

Kana transcription: ジョージャ／じょーじゃ

Purely phonetic transcription: 助王示亜　女王児雅
序追治阿　叙欧慈唖　徐往侍阿　如鴬辞雅
情示亜　嬢寺唖　蒸士雅　常時唖　醸持阿

Purely denotative transcription: See George

Phonetic & denotative transcription: 地用者 = one who makes use of the land = hence a "man of the earth, farmer"; 地養慈雅 = one who enriches the land well = hence a "man of the earth, farmer"; 地擁者 = one who takes care of land = hence a "man of the earth, farmer"; 壌治雅 = one who cultivates and rules the soil = a farmer."

Phonetic & eulogistic transcription: 治養者 = one who rules and feeds people; 慈湧姐 = a woman from whom benevolence springs; 値擁者 = one who protects the prices = a merchant; 地要者 = one who needs land; 情者 = a kindhearted one= sweetheart.

Attention-getting transcription: 侍酔者 = a drunken samurai; 治羊児雅 = a child who controls sheep smartly = a smart shepherd child; 情事雅 = an elegant love affair; 冗事唖 = a joking matter.

Gerald

(m) Old German, compound of "spear" and "rule" (EGW)

Kana transcription: ジェラルド／じぇらるど

Purely phonetic transcription: 寺等瑠度　時羅琉土
字螺流怒　次良漏奴　辞羅琉土　地良留努

Purely denotative transcription: 槍統治 = spear and rule, *yari tochi*; 鎗政治 = spear and rule, *yari seiji*; 扠支配 = spear and rule, *yasu shihai*.

Phonetic & denotative transcription: 治等留土 = to rule people and keep them on the land = hence "rule."

Phonetic & eulogistic transcription: 慈等流度 = one who is frequently benevolent to people; 馳裸留奴 = one who serves meals to naked people; 持良留努 = one who makes an effort to stay good.

Attention-getting transcription: 寺裸留奴 = a temple where naked fellows live; 示裸留努 = one who tries to show his naked body.

Gilbert

(m) Germanic, compound of "pledge" and "bright" (GRS)

Kana transcription: ギルバート／ぎるばーと

Purely phonetic transcription: 議留馬都　技漏羽土　儀硫場渡　岐流芭徒　宜琉魔杜　犠瑠磨塗

Purely denotative transcription: 誓明晰 = pledge and bright, *chikai meiseki*; 誓門裏褥明細 = pledge and bright, *chikai meisai*; 約束明瞭 = pledge and bright, *yakusoku meiryo*.

Phonetic & denotative transcription: 義留磨雅図 = an elegant picture that depicts duty and remains polished = hence "bright"; 儀留馬雅杜 = to carry out the obligation of keeping horses well in the forest = hence "pledge"; 曦流磨雅都 = a brilliant city where sun light pours in = hence "bright."

Phonetic & eulogistic transcription: 侍留馬雅頭 = a samurai chief who keeps an elegant horse; 慈留馬雅頭 = an elegant knight leader who is benevolent.

Attention-getting transcription: 戯流頗雅頭 = an extremely elegant boss of playboys.

Glen

(m) Surname, which originally indicated one who lived in a valley (LDWG)

Kana transcription: グレン／ぐれん

Purely phonetic transcription: 具連　寓煉　虞恋　仇練　倶漣　偶簾

Purely denotative transcription: 谷住人 = a person who lives in a valley, *tani-jumin*; 谷間住民 = inhabitants in the valley, *kokukanjumin*; 峡谷住人 = inhabitants in the valley, *kyokokujunin*.

Phonetic & denotative transcription: 隅漣 = the intersection joining two waves = hence a "valley."

Phonetic & eulogistic transcription: 共憐 = ones who are mutually sympathetic; 救恋 = a love saver; 救蓮 = one who saves the lotus; 具憐 = one who bears a feeling of sympathy.

Attention-getting transcription: 愚恋 = a stupid love; 仇恋 = a rival in love; 愚練 = stupid training; 求恋 = a love hunter.

Gloria
(f) Latin, "glory" (EGW)

Kana transcription: グローリア／ぐろーりあ

Purely phonetic transcription: 具路右利亜　偶老理阿 寓浪離蛙　倶朗麗阿　遇篭哩亜　仇廊麗婀

Purely denotative transcription: 光栄 = glory, *koei*; 名誉 = glory, *meiyo*; 栄光 = glory, *eiko*; 華麗 = glory, *karei*; 壮麗 = glory, *sorei*.

Phonetic & denotative transcription: 遇良礼雅 = to treat well, courteously and elegantly = hence "glory"; 具朗理雅 = to be endowed with cheerfulness, intelligence and elegance = "glory."

Phonetic & eulogistic transcription: 救狼狸亜 = one who saves Asian wolves and badgers; 具慮利雅 = one who is endowed with carefulness, cleverness and elegance; 遇老麗雅 = one who treats old people nicely and elegantly.

Attention-getting transcription: 愚老狸亜 = a stupid old Asian badger; 紅露尾狸雅 = an elegant badger with a pink tail.

Gordon
(m) Old English, "spacious hill"; "three-cornered hill" (ECS)

Kana transcription: ゴードン／ごーどん

Purely phonetic transcription: 剛鈍　号丼　豪曇 強遁　合呑　劫遁　郷曇

Purely denotative transcription: 大岡 = a big hill, *ooka*; 広岡 = a spacious hill, *hirooka*; 広大丘 = a spacious hill, *kodai-kyu* or 三隅岡 = a three-cornered hill, *mitsumi oka*; 三角丘 = *sankakukyu*.

Phonetic & denotative transcription: 豪土雲 = a spacious land with a cloud high overhead = hence a "hill."

Phonetic & eulogistic transcription: 豪呑 = a heavy drinker; 劫努員 = one who makes eternal efforts; 昂怒雲 = a cumulonimbus cloud.

Attention-getting transcription: 豪鈍 = a extremely dull person; 豪貪 = an avaricious fellow.

Grace
(f) Latin, "thanks, thanksgiving" (especially to the gods) (HS)

Kana transcription: グレース／ぐれーす

Purely phonetic transcription: 具令位巣　倶礼寿　偶麗洲　仇霊寿　蕚鈴須　虞嶺素　救隷主

Purely denotative transcription: 感謝 = thanks, *kansha*; 謝意 = gratitude, *shai*; 万謝 = thanks, *bansha*; 鳴謝 = thanks, *meinsha*; 多謝 = thanks, *tasha*.

Phonetic & denotative transcription: 共礼意守 = to intend to give thanks = hence "thanks."

Phonetic & eulogistic transcription: 具麗威素 = one who is endowed with grace, dignity and simplicity; 求礼医寿 = a doctor who seeks to be courteous and long-living; 厚麗子 = a child with a lot of grace; 救隷寿 = one who saves an aging slave; 遇霊慰司 = an official who treats and consoles spirits well.

Attention-getting transcription: 愚麗子 = a stupid, but elegant child; 具霊手 = a ghost with hands.

Graham
(m) Surname, originally a Scottish place name (EGW)

Kana transcription: グラハム／ぐらはむ

Purely phonetic transcription: 具羅刃無　救良派務　虞等覇武　仇螺琶舞　偶良覇夢　遇羅波霧

Purely denotative transcription: 蘇格蘭地名 = a Scottish place name, *sukkotorando chimei*.

Phonetic & eulogistic transcription: 救等覇無 = one who saves people without conquering them; 仇良覇武 = a good revenging samurai who is victorious; 救裸派務 = one who saves naked people; 厚良伯務 = an extremely good count; 遇良覇務 = a conqueror in charge of treating the defeated well.

Attention-getting transcription: 愚螺波夢 = a stupid shell dreaming in the wave; 愚騾歯無 = a stupid toothless mule; 共蘿葉舞 = ivy leaves dancing together.

Greg
(m) Pet form of Gregory (LDWG); see Gregory

Kana transcription: グレッグ／ぐれっぐ

Purely phonetic transcription: 具霊救　偶令紅
仇例遇　遇例共　寓嶺求　虞鈴球　救礼偶

Purely denotative transcription: See Gregory

Phonetic & denotative transcription: 具励救 = one who tries to save = hence "a watchman."

Phonetic & eulogistic transcription: 求礼具 = one who seeks to master the art of courtesy; 救霊求 = a spirit which seeks a relief; 遇礼仇 = one who treats his enemy with courtesy.

Attention-getting transcription: 求霊仇 = one who seeks revenge on a ghost; 愚霊救 = one who saves a stupid ghost.

Gregory
(m) Latin, "vigilant," hence "watchman" (WNWD)

Kana transcription: グレゴリー／ぐれごりー

Purely phonetic transcription: 具霊御理位
偶令御利異　仇例禦里意　遇例悟吏委
寓嶺後令　虞鈴醐霊・救礼悟励

Purely denotative transcription: 用心 = vigilant, *yojin*; 警戒 = vigilant, *keikai*; 夜警 = night-watching, *yakei* or 警備員 = a watchman, *yakei*; 守衛 = a watchman, *shuei*.

Phonetic & denotative transcription: 具励護裡 = one who uses equipment to defend the interior of a home = hence "a watchman."

Phonetic & eulogistic transcription: 具礼悟領 = a president endowed with courtesy and insight; 救励護霊 = one who makes efforts to save and protect (his ancestors') spirits; 遇礼語麗 = one who offers courteous and elegant words.

Attention-getting transcription: 共霊碁狸 = a badger which plays chess with a ghost; 愚霊護狸 = a stupid ghost which protects a badger.

Guy

(m) Germanic, "sensible"; "leader"; "wood" (ECS)

Kana transcription: ガイ／がい

Purely phonetic transcription: 賀位　牙伊　伽偉
我異　雅医　臥尉　苛移　駕医　我意

Purely denotative transcription: 賢明 = sensible, *kenmei*;
分別 = sensible, *bunbetsu*; 敏感 = sensible, *binkan* or 指導者 = a
leader, *shidosha*; 首領 = a leader, *shuryo* or 木材 = wood, *mokuzai*;
材木 = wood, *zaimoku*.

Phonetic & denotative transcription: 雅意 = elegant will = hence
"sensible"; 苛威 = one who is harsh and terrifying/menacing =
hence a "leader"; 芽偉 = great sprouting = hence "wood."

Phonetic & eulogistic transcription: 雅位 = one who is in an elegant
position; 牙威 = threatening tusks; 雅医 = an elegant doctor; 駕医
= a mounted doctor; 賀医 = a joyful doctor.

Attention-getting transcription: 餓猪 = a starving boar; 鵞葦 = a
goose in the reeds; 臥医 = a sick doctor; 駕猪 = a wild boar rider.

Harold

(m) Old English, compound of "army" and
"power" (GRS)

Kana transcription: ハロルド／はろるど

Purely phonetic transcription: 覇路流度　伯露瑠努
顔慮留土　芭良琉藤

Purely denotative transcription: 戦力 = army and power,
senryoku; 武力 = army and power, *buryoku*; 軍力 = army and
power, *gunryoku*.

Phonetic & denotative transcription: 覇虜留度 = to conquer often
to keep prisoners = hence "army and power."

Phonetic & eulogistic transcription: 顔慮留怒 = one who is
extremely careful to withhold anger; 伯朗流努 = a duke who tries
to be cheerful; 芭路留童 = a child who stays in a flower-covered
lane; 覇虜留奴 = a conqueror who keeps prisoners as slaves.

Attention-getting transcription: 歯露留怒 = one who is angry
showing his teeth; 波浪流怒 = roaring waves.

81

Harriet
(f) Feminine form of Henry (LDWG); see Henry

Kana transcription: ハリエット／はりえっと

Purely phonetic transcription: 覇理江杜　頗利絵登
波吏慧頭　破裏恵都　伯麗衣徒　芭令衛妬
巴霊会堵　刃励兄渡　派礼懐途

Purely denotative transcription: See Henry

Phonetic & denotative transcription: 把令慧頭 = an wise boss who controls the law = hence a "ruler"; 覇令衛人 = one who holds hegemony over all law affairs and defends the law = hence a "ruler."

Phonetic & eulogistic transcription: 覇理恵統 = a conqueror who rules with wisdom and benevolence; 頗利恵徒 = an extremely clever and benevolent person; 頗利慧頭 = an extremely wise head; 頗麗衣人 = a person who wears extremely beautiful clothes.

Attention-getting transcription: 播狸餌渡 = one who gives feed to badgers; 頗璃偉賭 = one who gambles for a very great gem.

Harry
(m) Normal colloquial form of Henry (LDWG); see Henry

Kana transcription: ハリー／はりー

Purely phonetic transcription: 覇理医　頗利異
波吏位　破裏尉　伯麗　芭令　巴霊　刃励

Purely denotative transcription: See Henry

Phonetic & denotative transcription: 把令 = one who controls the law = hence a "ruler"; 覇令 = one who holds hegemony over all law affairs = hence a "ruler."

Phonetic & eulogistic transcription: 覇理威 = a wise and dignified conqueror; 歯麗医 = a doctor whose teeth are elegant; 頗利異 = one who is extremely and unusually clever; 伯麗 = an elegant duke; 頗励 = one who makes extraordinary efforts.

Attention-getting transcription: 歯狸威 = a badger with threatening teeth; 頗璃偉 = a very great gem; 歯離医 = a toothless doctor.

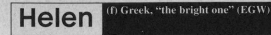

Helen
(f) Greek, "the bright one" (EGW)

Kana transcription: ヘレン／へれん
Purely phonetic transcription: 戸連　陛恋　経宴
減縁　併聯　兵憐　平漣
Purely denotative transcription: 聡明婦人 = a bright
woman, *somei fujin*; 賢明婦女 = a bright woman, *kenmei fujo*; 英
明麗人 = a bright woman, *eimei reijin*; 聡悟令夫人 = a bright
woman, *sogo reifujin*.

Phonetic & denotative transcription: 炳恋 = a bright love, a shining
love; 陛恋 = a royal love.

Phonetic & eulogistic transcription: 並蓮 = a series of lotuses; 陛蓮
= a royal lotus; 瓶蓮 = a lotus in a vase.

Attention-getting transcription: 並恋 = double love; 弊恋 = broken
heart; 閉恋 = a secret love; 聘恋 = one who invites love, hence a
love hunter; 批恋 = criticized love, a forbidden love.

Henry
**(m) Old German, compound of "house," "home"
and ruler" (EGW)**

Kana transcription: ヘンリー／へんりー
Purely phonetic transcription: 変理医　偏利異　編
吏位　返裏尉　遍麗　辺令　片霊　篇励　返礼
Purely denotative transcription: 家屋支配人 = house
and ruler, *kaoku shihaisha*; 戸庭統治者 = home and ruler, *totei
tochisha*; 国内支配者 = home and ruler, *kokunai shihaisha*.

Phonetic & denotative transcription: 鞭令 = one who issues strict
orders = hence a "ruler"; 編令 = one who issues laws = hence a
"ruler"; 変令 = one who modifies laws = hence a "ruler."

Phonetic & eulogistic transcription: 返礼医 = a doctor who repays
his patient's thanks; 弁麗 = one who makes an elegant speech.

Attention-getting transcription: 変狸威 = a strange arrogant badger;
変璃偉 = a great strange gem.

Herbert

(m) Germanic, compound of "army" and "bright, famous" (GRS)

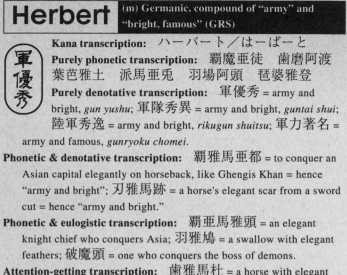

Kana transcription: ハーバート／はーばーと

Purely phonetic transcription: 覇魔亜徒　歯磨阿渡
葉芭雅士　派馬亜兎　羽場阿頭　琶婆雅登

Purely denotative transcription: 軍優秀 = army and
bright, *gun yushu*; 軍隊秀異 = army and bright, *guntai shui*;
陸軍秀逸 = army and bright, *rikugun shuitsu*; 軍力著名 =
army and famous, *gunryoku chomei*.

Phonetic & denotative transcription: 覇雅馬亜都 = to conquer an
Asian capital elegantly on horseback, like Ghengis Khan = hence
"army and bright"; 刃雅馬跡 = a horse's elegant scar from a sword
cut = hence "army and bright."

Phonetic & eulogistic transcription: 覇亜馬雅頭 = an elegant
knight chief who conquers Asia; 羽雅鳩 = a swallow with elegant
feathers; 破魔頭 = one who conquers the boss of demons.

Attention-getting transcription: 歯雅馬杜 = a horse with elegant
teeth in the forest; 頗罵阿兎 = an African rabbit which shouts.

Hillary

(f) Latin, "cheerful" (LDWG)

Kana transcription: ヒラリー／ひらりー

Purely phonetic transcription: 日等利異　比羅理医
陽良麗　秘螺理位　妃羅吏伊　飛等梨意

Purely denotative transcription: 快活 = cheerful, *kaikatsu*;
活発 = cheerful, *kappatsu*; 上機嫌 = cheerful, *jokigen*; 陽気 =
cheerful, *yoki*.

Phonetic & denotative transcription: 陽裸麗 = a cheerful naked
beauty = hence "cheerful"; 陽羅麗衣 = cheerful in elegant silk
clothes = hence "cheerful."

Phonetic & eulogistic transcription: 妃良利威 = a good, clever and
dignified princess; 陽裸麗 = a naked beauty who is sunbathing; 斐
良利医 = a beautiful, good and clever female doctor.

Attention-getting transcription: 日裸霊 = a sunbathing ghost; 疲騾
里蓁 = a tired sick mule in the village.

Horace

(m) Latin, "timekeeper" (ECS)

Kana transcription: ホーレス／ほーれす

Purely phonetic transcription: 方礼洲　報霊酸
豊励寿　奉令須　法例素　宝麗巣　砲伶諏

Purely denotative transcription: 時間記録人 = a time-keeper, *jikan kirokunin*; 時間記録係 = a timekeeper, *jikan kirokusha*; 計時係 = a timekeeper, *jikei kakari*; 拍子係 = a time-keeper, *hyoshi kakari*.

Phonetic & denotative transcription: 保励数 = one who tries to keep numbers = hence a "timekeeper"; 報零司 = an official who announces the zero hour = hence a "timekeeper."

Phonetic & eulogistic transcription: 豊麗主 = a rich and elegant master; 法令守 = one who guards the law.

Attention-getting transcription: 鯆礼寿 = a long-living courteous dolphin; 彷霊周 = a wandering ghost; 泡戻終 = a thing which dissipates into bubbles.

Howard

(m) Old English, "sword"; "guardian"; "hedge warden" (ECS)

Kana transcription: ハワード／はわーど

Purely phonetic transcription: 這和亜土　波輪雅度
琶環阿努　覇倭唖怒

Purely denotative transcription: 刀 = a sword, *katana*; 剣 = a sword, *katana*; 刀剣 = a sword, *katana* or 守護者 = a guardian, *shugosha* or 生垣管理人 = a hedge warden, *ikegaki kanrinin*.

Phonetic & denotative transcription: 葉憂和雅努 = one who takes care of leaves and keeps them beautiful = "a hedge warden"; 刃有和努 = a sword which strives to keep the peace = hence a "sword."

Phonetic & eulogistic transcription: 覇和夥土 = one who conquers a lot of land in a peaceful manner; 頗話唖怒 = one who often talks, laughs and gets angry.

Attention-getting transcription: 頗蛙話怒 = a frog that talks too much in anger; 伯雅羽憧 = a count who adores beautiful birds.

Hubert

(m) Old German, compound of "heart," "mind" and "bright" (EGW)

Kana transcription: ヒューバート／ひゅーばーと

Purely phonetic transcription: 比憂馬阿登　批友罵妬 陽優場雅渡　被悠芭阿都　飛勇鳩　肥憂婆妬

Purely denotative transcription: 心照映 = heart and bright, *shin shoei*; 心晃耀 = heart and bright, *shin koyo*; 心情陽気 = heart and bright, *shinjo yoki*; 精神明快 = soul and bright, *seishin meika*.

Phonetic & denotative transcription: 陽有磨雅度 = to polish something so that it becomes as bright as the sun = hence "bright."

Phonetic & eulogistic transcription: 陽裕馬雅杜 = an elegant horse in the forest which gets a lot of sun light; 飛勇鳩 = a brave flying dove; 秘悠磨頭 = an well-off person who secretly polishes his head.

Attention-getting transcription: 批湧罵頭 = a boss who condemns and criticizes continuously; 鼻有磨頭 = a boss with a shiny nose.

Hugh

(m) Old German, "mind, soul, thought" (LDWG)

Kana transcription: ヒュウ／ひゅう

Purely phonetic transcription: 比優　陽右　悲憂 飛遊　批悠　避佑　秘誘　斐有　火幽　肥裕

Purely denotative transcription: 心 = mind, *kokoro*; 精神 = soul, *seishin* or 魂 = soul, *tamashi*; 精魂 = soul, *seikon* or 思想 = thought, *shiso*.

Phonetic & denotative transcription: 批湧 = a passionate sense of right and wrong = hence "mind, soul, thought."

Phonetic & eulogistic transcription: 陽優 = the tender sun; 陽勇 = the brave sun; 飛雄 = a flying hero; 斐悠 = one who is handsome and well-off; 妃友 = a friend of the princess.

Attention-getting transcription: 日憂 = the melancholy sun; 疲憂 = one who is tired and blue; 卑友 = a indecent friend; 肥憂 = one who is fat and therefore melancholy.

Humphrey

(m) Germanic, "giant"; "peace" (ECS)

Kana transcription: ハンフリー／はんふりー

Purely phonetic transcription: 判富理意　半符利医　反夫里異　版父離位　扶不李委　犯不裡偉

Purely denotative transcription: 巨大平和 = giant, peace, *kyodai heiwa*; 巨人和平 = giant, peace, *kyojin wahei*; 偉人平安 = giant, peace, *ijin heian*; 偉大安泰 = giant, peace, *idai antai*.

Phonetic & denotative transcription: 播富励 = to try to spread fortunes = hence "peace"; 叛不令 = an anti-riot law = hence "peace."

Phonetic & eulogistic transcription: 範夫礼 = a courteous model husband; 繁父怜 = a prosperous intelligent father; 搬輔励 = one who brings help and encouragement.

Attention-getting transcription: 叛婦励 = one who encourages rebelling women; 煩怖霊 = a disturbing and horrifying ghost.

Irene

(f) Greek, Latin, "messenger of peace" (HS)

Kana transcription: アイレーン／あいれーん

Purely phonetic transcription: 阿委連　雅位憐　亜医聯　愛練　相恋　藍漣　哀蓮　挨簾　娃錬

Purely denotative transcription: 平和使者 = a messenger of peace, *heiwa shisha*; 和平伝令 = a messenger of peace, *wahei denrei*; 平安使 = a messenger of peace, *heian tsukai*.

Phonetic & denotative transcription: 愛連 = an alliance based on love (which brings "peace"; 愛練 = to train in love (thus to bring out "peace"); 愛憐 = love and sympathy = hence the basis for "peace."

Phonetic & eulogistic transcription: 藍蓮 = a purple lotus; 相恋 = a mutual love; 愛恋 = a love affair; 愛蓮 = a lovely lotus = 娃恋 = a beauty in love.

Attention-getting transcription: 愛漣 = light waves of love; 娃連 = a league of beauties; 哀恋 = a sad love; 蛙井恋 = a frog which makes love in a well; 鴉医連 = the league of crow doctors.

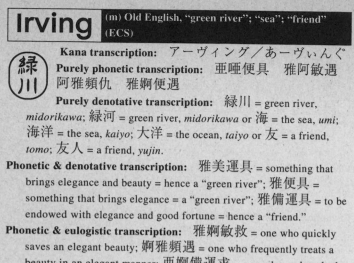

Irving

(m) Old English, "green river"; "sea"; "friend" (ECS)

緑川

Kana transcription: アーヴィング／あーゔぃんぐ

Purely phonetic transcription: 亜唖便具　雅阿敏遇
阿雅頻仇　雅婀便遇

Purely denotative transcription: 緑川 = green river,
midorikawa; 緑河 = green river, *midorikawa* or 海 = the sea, *umi*;
海洋 = the sea, *kaiyo*; 大洋 = the ocean, *taiyo* or 友 = a friend,
tomo; 友人 = a friend, *yujin*.

Phonetic & denotative transcription: 雅美運具 = something that
brings elegance and beauty = hence a "green river"; 雅便具 =
something that brings elegance = a "green river"; 雅備運具 = to be
endowed with elegance and good fortune = hence a "friend."

Phonetic & eulogistic transcription: 雅婀敏救 = one who quickly
saves an elegant beauty; 婀雅頻遇 = one who frequently treats a
beauty in an elegant manner; 亜婀備運求 = one who seeks a lucky
Asian beauty.

Attention-getting transcription: 亜蛙貧紅 = a poor pink Asian frog;
雅蛙頻救 = one who often saves elegant frogs.

Isabel

(f) Spanish/Portuguese form of Elizabeth (LDWG); see Elizabeth

慰部婁

Kana transcription: イザベル／いざべる

Purely phonetic transcription: 意座部留　偉坐辺流
威座琶漏　畏座辺瑠　慰部婁　永座辺琉

Purely denotative transcription: See Elizabeth

Phonetic & denotative transcription: 意座辺瑠 = an
eternally glittering wish = hence "oath of God"; 叡座迷流 =
providence which washes away our delusions = hence "oath of God."

Phonetic & eulogistic transcription: 英座辺留 = permanently
lingering glory; 恵座部留 = benevolence which stays in the village;
栄座部留 = a village where prosperity stays.

Attention-getting transcription: 猪坐辺瑠 = a badger which sits
besides the gems; 医坐部留 = a doctor in the village.

Isaac (m) Hebrew, "he laughs," or "the laughter" (ECS)

Kana transcription: アイザック／あいざっく

Purely phonetic transcription: 阿医座句　雅位坐久
藍座玖　相坐久　哀挫句　愛咲　娃索

Purely denotative transcription: 彼笑 = He laughs, *kasho*
or 笑 = laughter, *warai*; 発笑 = laughter, *hassho*; 破笑 = laughter,
hasho; 解笑 = laughter, *kaisho*.

Phonetic & denotative transcription: 雅笑座公 = a duke who sits
laughing elegantly = hence "he laughs"; 愛挫苦 = love conquers
pain = hence "he laughs"; 挨策 = salutation is the best policy; 愛咲
= love blooms; 娃咲 = pretty girls bloom.

Phonetic & eulogistic transcription: 雅慰策 = one who plans to
console elegantly; 愛策 = one who plans for love; 愛咲 = a
blooming love; 娃索 = one who looks for a beauty; 愛作 = one who
makes love; 相座久 = ones who sit together forever.

Attention-getting transcription: 娃挫苦 = a disheartened beauty
suffering pain; 蛙偉座宮 = a great frog seated in the palace; 愛裂
= a love which breaks = hence a broken love.

Jack (m) Pet form of John (EGW); Hebrew, "gracious gift of God" (ECS)

Kana transcription: ジャック／じゃっく

Purely phonetic transcription: 慈家苦　侍矢功
治哉究　滋夜供　寺屋公

Purely denotative transcription: See John

Phonetic & denotative transcription: 慈矢供 = to provide
a benevolent arrow = hence "Jehovah has favored"; 慈家救 =
benevolence which saved the house = "gracious gift of God."

Phonetic & eulogistic transcription: 侍矢救 = a samurai who saves
people with his arrows; 慈家公 = a benevolent prince; 持野駒 =
one who owns a wild horse; 士邪駆 = a samurai who drives out
evil.

Attention-getting transcription: 侍夜駈 = a samurai who runs at
night; 慈野狗 = a benevolent wild dog.

Jacob

(m) Hebrew, "may God protect"; "replacement goods" (ECS)

Kana transcription: ジェイコブ／じぇいこぶ

Purely phonetic transcription: 時影故部　寺栄個歩
自英古分　事永昆布　治叡庫撫　字誇舞

Purely denotative transcription: 神守護 = God's protection, *kami shugo* or 代替品 = replacement goods, *daigaihin*; 代用品 = replacement goods, *daiyohin*; 代行者 = replacement (person), *daikosha*.

Phonetic & denotative transcription: 治恵護輔 = benevolence which cures, protects and helps = "may God protect"; 慈恵許輔 = benevolence permits to help = "may God protect"; 示恵乞輔 = to ask for benevolent help = "may God protect."

Phonetic & eulogistic transcription: 治衛誇武 = a proud samurai who rules and defends; 慈恵鼓舞 = one who encourages benevolence; 侍慧護輔 = a wise samurai who protects and helps; 自衛雇武 = one who defends himself by employing warriors.

Attention-getting transcription: 侍会虎撫 = a samurai who meets and pets a tiger; 示餌狐捕 = one who shows bait to a fox in order to catch it = hence a fox hunter.

Jacqueline

(f) French feminine diminutive of Jacob (EGW); see Jacob

Kana transcription: ジャックリーン／じゃっくりーん

Purely phonetic transcription: 時夜駈離引　尼夜供鈴
示野駈林　慈家供輪　持矢救倫

Purely denotative transcription: See Jacob

Phonetic & denotative transcription: 慈矢救臨 = a benevolent arrow of salvation = hence "may god protect"; 邪駆倫 = ethics which drive evil out = "may God protect."

Phonetic & eulogistic transcription: 児哉駈林 = a child who begins to run around in the forest; 尼爺救林 = a nun who saves an old man in the forest; 邪苦臨 = one who stands against evils and hardships.

Attention-getting transcription: 蛇駈林 = a snake which runs in the forest; 邪狗淋 = an evil dog which is lonely.

James

(m) Late Latin, an altered from of Jacob, ultimately from Hebrew (LDWG); see Jacob

Kana transcription: ジェームス／じぇーむす

Purely phonetic transcription: 時影夢蘇　寺栄武子　自英霧寿　事永舞主　地泳務州　侍影蕪素

Purely denotative transcription: See Jacob

Phonetic & denotative transcription: 慈恵務守 = benevolence in charge of protection = hence "may God protect"; 示恵武守 = showing benevolence to protect by arms = hence "may God protect."

Phonetic & eulogistic transcription: 侍英務守 = a bright samurai in charge of protecting; 自栄夢蘇 = one whose dream of prospering has come true automatically; 慈盈武主 = a samurai master filled with benevolence.

Attention-getting transcription: 侍会舞雛 = a samurai who meets a dancing fledgling; 示餌鸚素 = one who shows baits to a simple parrot = hence a parrot hunter; 児泳務主 = a manager in charge of swimming kids; 爺夢寿 = an old man who dreams of longevity.

Jane

(f) Hebrew, "gracious gift of God" (ECS); feminine form of John (GRS); see John

Kana transcription: ジェーン／じぇーん

Purely phonetic transcription: 時恵遠　寺慧園　自恵縁　事江援　地重炎　侍衛演　治叡宴　馳宴

Purely denotative transcription: See John

Phonetic & denotative transcription: 示恵演 = to show benevolence = hence "Jehovah has favored"; 慈恵援 = benevolent assistance = hence "Jehovah has favored."

Phonetic & eulogistic transcription: 慈栄羨 = benevolence and prosperity which others envy; 示恵艶 = one who shows benevolence and female charms; 尼慧員 = a wise nun; 自衛援 = one who defends himself.

Attention-getting transcription: 尼会縁 = a nun who meets her acquaintances; 慈会猿 = a monkey which meets benevolence; 尼懐羨 = a jealous nun.

Janice

(f) Diminutive of Jane (LDWG); see John

Kana transcription: ジャニス／じゃにす

Purely phonetic transcription: 慈家仁寿　侍矢尼主
治哉児守　滋夜丹司　時野弐蘇　寺哉爾洲

Purely denotative transcription:　See John

Phonetic & denotative transcription:　慈矢尼守 = the
benevolent arrow which has protected a nun = hence "Jehovah
has favored"; 邪矢児守 = to protect a child from an evil arrow =
hence "Jehovah has favored."

Phonetic & eulogistic transcription:　寺家尼寿 = a long-living nun
in the temple; 慈射児素 = a simple child who radiates benevolence;
慈家尼主 = a benevolent chief nun.

Attention-getting transcription:　飼屋尼雛 = a nun who brings up
fledglings in the room; 馳爺尼主 = a chief nun who serves dishes
to an old man.

Jason

**(m) Hebrew, "Jehovah saves"; "God is generous"
(LDWG)**

Kana transcription: ジェーソン／じぇーそん

Purely phonetic transcription: 字江村　治絵孫
地柄損　事慧尊　侍重遜　自恵存　寺衛寸

Purely denotative transcription: 神救済 = God saves,
kami kyusai; 神寛容 = God is generous, *kami kanyo*; 神寛
宏 = God is generous, *kami kanko*; 神寛裕 = God is
generous, *kami kanyu*.

Phonetic & denotative transcription:　慈衛損 = benevolence protects
us from our losses = hence "God saves"; 慈衛孫 = benevolence
protects grandsons = hence "God saves."

Phonetic & eulogistic transcription:　示恵尊 = one who shows
respectable benevolence; 自営孫 = a grandson who runs his own
business; 自衛存 = one who defends himself to exist.

Attention-getting transcription:　似餌鱒 = a lure for a trout; 自泳
樽 = a self-swimming barrel; 似栄孫 = a grandson who pretends
prosperity; 侍営損 = a samurai who suffers business losses.

Jean
(f) Scottish feminine form of John (GRS); see John

Kana transcription: ジーン／じーん

Purely phonetic transcription: 慈威員　寺偉音
治畏隠　尼慰韻　侍医院　馳院

Purely denotative transcription: See John

Phonetic & denotative transcription: 慈慰引 = to console with benevolence = hence "Jehovah has favored"; 慈施蔭 = to provide benevolence secretly = hence "Jehovah has favored."

Phonetic & eulogistic transcription: 慈医員 = a benevolent doctor; 尼偉員 = a great nun; 児食員 = one who feeds children; 尼医姻 = a nun who marries a doctor.

Attention-getting transcription: 餌猪引 = one who lures a wild boar with bait = hence a wild boar hunter; 慈猪姻 = a benevolent wild boar who marries.

Jeff
(m) Pet form of Jeffrey (LDWG); see Jeffrey

Kana transcription: ジェフリー／じぇふりー

Purely phonetic transcription: 時府　字富　次符
辞父　地不　事賦　自豊　寺布　寺付　侍扶

Purely denotative transcription: See Jeffrey

Phonetic & denotative transcription: 侍否 = samurai denied = hence "peace"; 治富 = to rule in fortune = hence "peace."

Phonetic & eulogistic transcription: 侍富 = a rich samurai; 慈夫 = a benevolent husband; 児豊 = a rich child; 持婦 = one who has a wife = hence a married man; 治輔 = one who rules and helps.

Attention-getting transcription: 治婦 = one who cures women = hence a gynecologist; 侍怖 = a fearful samurai; 次婦 = one who chases after women; 示怖 = one who threatens.

Jeffrey (m) Old German, compound of "peace" and another unknown element (LDWG)

Kana transcription: ジェフリー／じぇふりー

Purely phonetic transcription: 時府理偉　字富李位　次符里威　辞父利畏　児豊理　侍布里　磁撫璃

Purely denotative transcription: 平穏 = peace, *heian*; 太平 = peace, *taihei*; 平和 = peace, *heiwa*; 和平 = peace, *wahei*.

Phonetic & denotative transcription: 治豊里為 = to rule such that the village may become rich = hence "peace"; 慈富礼維 = to maintain benevolence, fortune and courtesy = hence "peace."

Phonetic & eulogistic transcription: 慈富理威 = one who is benevolent, rich, wise and dignified; 士豊理 = a rich and intelligent samurai; 児富麗 = a rich and handsome child.

Attention-getting transcription: 次婦麗 = one who chases after beautiful women; 侍怖吏 = a samurai who fears officials.

Jennifer (f) Celtic, white fair lady (ECS)

Kana transcription: ジェニファー／じぇにふぁー

Purely phonetic transcription: 自荷婦亜　慈仁豊雅　事尼富阿　侍丹府亜　磁尼芙阿　治爾布雅

Purely denotative transcription: 色白美人 = a white fair lady, *irojiro bijin*; 色白婦人 = a white fair lady, *irojiro fujin*.

Phonetic & denotative transcription: 慈児芙婀 = a tenderhearted young beauty who is as white as a rose mallow plant = hence "a white fair lady"; 示新膚婀 = a beauty showing a new skin = hence "a white fair lady."

Phonetic & eulogistic transcription: 慈尼富雅 = a benevolent, rich and elegant nun; 治仁婦雅 = a benevolent and elegant lady who rules 児仁豊唖 = a benevolent, rich child who is laughing.

Attention-getting transcription: 銭撫婀 = a beauty who strokes her money affectionately; 侍尼怖雅 = an elegant nun who is afraid of samurai; 持児否婀 = a beauty who refuses to have babies.

Jeremy

(m) Hebrew, "may Jehovah raise up, exalt" (EGW)

Kana transcription: ジェレミー／じぇれみー
Purely phonetic transcription: 治令実絵　自霊三重　地例未医　侍嶺御位　慈霊身偉　爾礼実威
Purely denotative transcription: 神高揚 = God raises up, *kami koyo*; 神高貴 = God is exalted, *kami koki*; 神高遠 = God is exalted, *kami koen*; 神高尚 = God is exalted, *kami koki*; 神賞揚 = God raises up, *kami shoyo*.

Phonetic & denotative transcription: 慈霊御威 = may the benevolent spirit be dignified = hence "may Jehovah raise up."

Phonetic & eulogistic transcription: 示礼身医 = a doctor who shows courtesy; 慈怜美威 = one who is benevolent, wise, handsome and dignified; 侍礼身偉 = a great samurai who is courteous; 自励身移 = one who trains himself to change.

Attention-getting transcription: 侍霊魅威 = a charming and dignified ghost of a samurai; 値零子猪 = a wild boar child that has no value at all.

Jerry

(m) Pet form of Jeremy (LDWG); see Jeremy

Kana transcription: ジェリー／じぇりー
Purely phonetic transcription: 治慧理威　自衛利医　地恵璃井　侍衣麗畏　慈会裏位　寺恵吏食
Purely denotative transcription: See Jeremy
Phonetic & denotative transcription: 慈叡利畏 = to be benevolent, intelligent, clever and respectful = hence "may Jehovah raise up."

Phonetic & eulogistic transcription: 侍慧理偉 = a great wise samurai; 慈重利医 = a kind and extremely clever doctor; 児英麗威 = a bright, elegant and dignified child; 示恵吏畏 = a respectful official who shows benevolence.

Attention-getting transcription: 侍恵霊 = a samurai who is benevolent to a ghost; 持慧零 = one who has no wisdom at all; 児餌鯉井 = a child who gives bait to the carp in the well.

Jesse
(m) Hebrew, "God is" (GRS)

Kana transcription: ジェッセ／じぇっせ

Purely phonetic transcription: 地背　自瀬　治施　爾勢　慈世　侍猷　示世

Purely denotative transcription: 神在 = God is, *kami ari*; 神存在 = God is, *kami sonzai*; 神実在 = God is, *kami jitsuzai*; 神実存 = God is, *kami jitsuzon*.

Phonetic & denotative transcription: 慈慧勢 = benevolence and providence that prospers = hence "God is"; 慈叡施 = to provide benevolence and providence = hence "God is"; 示聖 = to show holiness = hence "God is."

Phonetic & eulogistic transcription: 治世 = one who rules the world; 侍栄勢 = a prosperous and powerful samurai; 慈正 = one who is benevolent and right; 持誠 = one who is sincere.

Attention-getting transcription: 馳施 = one who provides dishes = a cook; 侍壊世 = a samurai who breaks the world; 次婿 = the next bridegroom.

Jimmy
(m) Pet form of James (LDWG); James/Jacob

Kana transcription: ジミー／じみー

Purely phonetic transcription: 慈魅威　侍身畏　児美医　自御偉　治実位

Purely denotative transcription: See James/Jacob

Phonetic & denotative transcription: 慈身慰 = benevolence which consoles a person = hence "may God protect"; 示深威 = to show profound dignity = hence "may God protect."

Phonetic & eulogistic transcription: 侍身偉 = a great samurai; 慈御医 = a benevolent doctor who is respectful; 児美異 = an extraordinarily cute child; 示深医 = a doctor who shows profundity.

Attention-getting transcription: 侍未威 = a samurai who is not dignified = hence a young samurai; 慈微医 = a doctor who has little benevolence; 児美猪 = a cute wild boar child.

Joan
(f) Feminine form of John (GRS); see John

除暗

Kana transcription: ジョン／じょん

Purely phonetic transcription: 助恩　叙温　序穏
除闇　如隠　序按　除暗　如案　恕行　汝安

Purely denotative transcription: See John

Phonetic & denotative transcription: 示誉恩 = to have shown honor and obligations = hence "Jehovah has favored"; 助雅運 = to help by bringing auspicious fortune = hence "Jehovah has favored"; 除暗 = to get rid of darkness = hence "Jehovah has favored"; 助安 = to help peace = hence "Jehovah has favored."

Phonetic & eulogistic transcription: 侍代怨 = a samurai's grudge which continues for generations; 持与運 = one who brings luck, or 助案 = one who helps planning; 女安 = a peaceful woman.

Attention-getting transcription: 示夜雲 = a cloud which appears at night; 侍夜運 = a samurai who moves at night; 似踊雲 = a cloud which looks like it is dancing = a dancing cloud; 女闇 = a woman in the dark; 薯鞍 = potatoes on the saddle.

Jocelyn
(f) Latin, Germanic, "merry"; "a Goth" (ECS)

愉快

Kana transcription: ジョセリン／じょせりん

Purely phonetic transcription: 女瀬隣　序施林
助世輪　叙勢厘　如背倫

Purely denotative transcription: 愉快 = merry, *yukai*; 陽気 = merry, *yoki*; 快活 = merry, *kaikatsu* or 蛮人 = a barbarian, *banjin,* as the Romans used to call the Goths.

Phonetic & denotative transcription: 情盛臨 = to show feelings fully = hence "merry."

Phonetic & eulogistic transcription: 女誓倫 = a woman who swears constancy; 情誠倫 = one who is kindhearted, sincere and ethical; 嬢正倫 = an ethically right girl.

Attention-getting transcription: 女勢輪 = a woman power circle; 嬢勢恋 = a girl whose love heats up.

John (m) Hebrew, "Jehovah has favored" (EGW)

Kana transcription: ジョン／じょん

Purely phonetic transcription: 助恩　叙温　序穏
除闇　如隠　恕御　汝怨

Purely denotative transcription: 神愛顧 = God's favor,
kami aiko; 神好意 = God's favor, *kami koi*; 神恩恵 = God's favor,
kami onkei; 神支持 = God's support, *kami shiji*.

Phonetic & denotative transcription: 慈預運 = to show continuing
benevolence = hence "Jehovah has favored"; 助運 = to help luck =
hence "Jehovah has favored"; 示誉恩 = to show honor and
obligation = hence "Jehovah has favored."

Phonetic & eulogistic transcription: 侍代怨 = a samurai's grudge
which continues for generations; 持与運 = one who brings luck; 慈
与運 = benevolence which gives luck.

Attention-getting transcription: 持夜運 = one who has luck at night;
似踊雲 = a cloud which looks like it is dancing = a dancing cloud.

Jonathan (m) Hebrew, "The Lord has given" (WNWD)

Kana transcription: ジョナサン／じょなさん

Purely phonetic transcription: 序名産　助菜参
所奈散　汝那山　叙名算　除難惨　女南讃

Purely denotative transcription: 神贈与 = God has given,
kami zoyo; 神授与 = God has given, *kami juyo*; 神贈呈 =
God has given, *kami zotei*;　主付与 = the Lord has given,
shu zoyo; 主捧呈 = the Lord has given, *shu hotei*.

Phonetic & denotative transcription: 譲納餐 = to have given supper
= our daily bread = hence "the Lord has given."

Phonetic & eulogistic transcription: 除難散 = one who gets rid of
bad fortune; 助名残 = one who helps names be known to the world;
情男燦 = a brilliant lover.

Attention-getting transcription: 女納讃 = one who gets girls by
praising them; 除娜散 = one who drives away beauties = an ugly
man.

Joseph
(m) Latin, Greek, Hebrew, "may He add" (WNWD)

Kana transcription: ジョセフ／じょせふ
Purely phonetic transcription: 所瀬府　女瀬富
序施不　助世父　叙勢符　如背豊　汝施賦
　　Purely denotative transcription: 増加 = increase, *zoka*; 追加 = addition, *tsuika*; 添加 = addition, *tenka*; 付加 = addition, *fuka*.

Phonetic & denotative transcription: 助世付 = to help the world to add = hence "may He add."

Phonetic & eulogistic transcription: 助世富 = one who helps the world become rich; 助税豊 = one who helps the tax revenues increase; 剰盛富 = one who is excessively rich.

Attention-getting transcription: 女勢怖 = one who is afraid of woman power; 女性撫 = a man who gropes woman = a playboy.

Josephine
(f) English feminine form of Joseph (HS); see Joseph

Kana transcription: ジョセフィン／じょせふぃん
Purely phonetic transcription: 所瀬府引　女瀬富姻
序施不隠　助世父院　叙勢符韻　如背豊音
Purely denotative transcription:　See Joseph

Phonetic & denotative transcription: 助世富引 = one who brings the world fortune = hence "may He add."

Phonetic & eulogistic transcription: 助妻豊引 = a helpful wife who brings riches; 女施夫引 = a woman who leads her husband; 女誠扶引 = a sincere woman who seeks help.

Attention-getting transcription: 女聖怖姻 = a holy woman who is afraid of marrying; 女清夫隠 = a pure woman who hides her husband; 女性膚引 = a woman with a charming skin.

Joshua

(m) Hebrew, "Jehovah saves"; "God is generous" (LDWG)

Kana transcription: ジョシュア／じょしゅあ

Purely phonetic transcription: 助主雅　汝首阿
徐手亜　除朱阿　叙種雅　恕酒阿　女守亜

Purely denotative transcription: 神救助 = God saves, *kami kyujo*; 神救済 = God saves, *kami kyusai*; 神救援 = God saves, *kami kyuen*; 神救護 = God saves, *kami kyugo* or 神寛大 = God is generous, *kami kandai*; 神寛容 = God is generous, *kami kanyo*; 神寛宏 = God is generous, *kami kanko*; 神寛裕 = God is generous, *kami kanyu*.

Phonetic & denotative transcription: 助主雅 = the Lord saves elegantly = hence "Jehovah saves."

Phonetic & eulogistic transcription: 除醜悪 = one who gets rid of ugly and bad matters; 助守婀 = one who guards a beauty; 助愁唖 = one who helps melancholy people laugh.

Attention-getting transcription: 女狩蛙 = a frog which hunts for women; 助痩鴉 = one who helps a thin crow; 女酒痴 = one pathologically obsessed with women and wine.

Joy

(f) The English noun seems to have been transferred into a name (GRS)

Kana transcription: ジョイ／じょい

Purely phonetic transcription: 助医　汝威　徐偉
除位　叙移　恕委　女意　如尉　徐畏

Purely denotative transcription: 欣喜 = joy, *kinki*; 歓喜 = joy, *kanki*; 喜悦 = joy, *kietsu*; 愉悦 = joy, *yuetsu*.

Phonetic & denotative transcription: 情懿 = a wonderful feeling = hence "joy"; 情偉 = a great feeling = hence "joy."

Phonetic & eulogistic transcription: 女医 = a female doctor; 女威 = a dignified woman; 助慰 = one who helps and consoles; 情医 = a warm-hearted doctor; 盛医 = a prospering doctor.

Attention-getting transcription: 女猪 = a female wild boar; 女易 = a female crystal gazer; 女尉 = a woman lieutenant.

Joyce
(f) Old French, "joyful, merry" (ECS)

Kana transcription: ジョイス／じょいす

Purely phonetic transcription: 女意州　序委巣　助位諏　叙畏須　如伊素　徐尉寿　除偉簾

Purely denotative transcription: 欣喜 = joy, *kinki*; 歓喜 = joy, *kanki*; 喜悦 = joy, *kietsu*; 愉悦 = joy, *yuetsu*; 悦喜 = joy, *etsuki*; 感喜 = joy, *kanki*; 愉快 = merry, *yukai*; 陽気 = merry, *yoki*.

Phonetic & denotative transcription: 情懿素 = a simply wonderful feeling = hence "joyful; merry."

Phonetic & eulogistic transcription: 女医主 = a female doctor chief; 女威寿 = a long-living dignified woman; 助慰司 = an official who helps and consoles; 情医子 = a warm-hearted doctor's child; 盛医蘇 = a doctor who revives to prosper.

Attention-getting transcription: 杖以守 = one who defends with a stick; 女囲酒 = a woman surrounded by wine = hence a bar hostess.

Judith
(f) Hebrew, "praise of the Lord"; "a Jewess" (HS)

Kana transcription: ジュデイス／じゅでいす

Purely phonetic transcription: 受出位巣　授弟偉寿　儒出威須　寿泥諏　綬弟須　樹出寿　呪弟諏

Purely denotative transcription: 神賛美 = the praise of God, *kami sanbi*; 主賛嘆 = the praise of the Lord, *kami santan* or 猶太娘 = a Jewess, *yuda musume*; 猶太女 = a Jewess, *yuda onna*.

Phonetic & denotative transcription: 従弟主 = a disciple of the Lord = "praise of the Lord"; 猶太秀 = a Jewish genius = a "Jewess."

Phonetic & eulogistic transcription: 獣帝寿 = a long-living animal queen; 従弟司 = an official who follows his younger brother; 充出寿 = one who has enjoyed longevity sufficiently; 従帝守 = one who follows and guards the emperor.

Attention-getting transcription: 樹出酒 = wine which comes out of a tree; 重泥巣 = a nest made of heavy mud.

Julia (f) Greek, "soft-haired or downy-cheeked" (HS)

Kana transcription: ジュリア／じゅりあ
Purely phonetic transcription: 樹里雅　授理阿
寿離亜　儒裏雅　綏履亜　呪裡阿　需麗亜
Purely denotative transcription: See Julian
Phonetic & denotative transcription: 柔麗婀 = a soft and
beautiful girl = hence "downy or soft hair."

Phonetic & eulogistic transcription: 寿吏雅 = an elegant long-living
official; 従理婀 = a beauty who follows reason; 柔利婀 = a soft
clever beauty.

Attention-getting transcription: 寿狸亜 = a long-living Asian
badger; 雛離鴉 = a fledgling which leaves the crow; 呪狸亜 = a
cursed Asian badger.

Julian (m) Latin, "downy-bearded; youthful" (ECS)

Kana transcription: ジュリアン／じゅりあん
Purely phonetic transcription: 樹里杏　授理鞍
寿離闇　儒裏安　綏履案　従裡行　需麗按
Purely denotative transcription: 産毛 = soft hair of a
baby, *ubuge*; 胎髪 = soft hair of a baby, *taihatsu*; 薄毛 = soft hair,
usuge; 軟毛 = soft hair, *nanmo*.

Phonetic & denotative transcription: 柔麗杏 = a soft beautiful
apricot = hence "downy or soft hair."

Phonetic & eulogistic transcription: 寿吏鞍 = a long-living official
in the saddle; 受利案 = one who plans to receive profits; 従理安
= one who follows reason to be safe; 就吏庵 = an official who
works at a vacation home; 珠麗鞍 = a saddle beautifully decorated
with gems.

Attention-getting transcription: 寿狸亜運 = a long-living, lucky
Asian badger; 雛離鴉雲 = a fledgling which gets separated from an
adult crow in the clouds; 呪狸闇 = a cursed Asian badger in the
dark.

Juliet 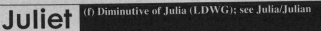 (f) Diminutive of Julia (LDWG); see Julia/Julian

Kana transcription: ジュリエット／じゅりえっと

Purely phonetic transcription: 樹里江渡　授理慧頭　寿離恵　儒裏衛都　綴履会杜　呪裡絵途

Purely denotative transcription: See Julia/Julian

Phonetic & denotative transcription: 柔裡異兎 = the unusually soft inside of a rabbit = "downy or soft hair."

Phonetic & eulogistic transcription: 寿理恵人 = a long-living, wise and benevolent person; 授利慧人 = one who is endowed with cleverness and intelligence; 従理恵度 = one who follows reason and benevolence.

Attention-getting transcription: 寿狸餌杜 = a long-living badger looking for food in the forest; 就離餌兎 = a rabbit which leaves its feed = hence a satisfied rabbit; 呪狸慧兎 = a badger which curses a wise rabbit.

June (f) The name of the month (EGW)

Kana transcription: ジューン／じゅーん

Purely phonetic transcription: 授宇運　樹右雲　寿雨均　儒憂雲　需羽運 or 授運　樹雲　寿均　儒雲　需運

Purely denotative transcription: 六月 = June, *rokugatsu*; 水無月 = June, *minatsuki*.

Phonetic & denotative transcription: 濡雨雲 = wet rain clouds which characterize the rainy month of June = hence "June."

Phonetic & eulogistic transcription: 慈優雲 = a benevolent graceful cloud; 寿運 = long-living luck; 授運 = one who is given good luck; 重雨雲 = accumulating rain clouds.

Attention-getting transcription: 似踊雲 = a dancing cloud; 自遊雲 = a cloud playing alone in the sky; 雛運 = a fledgling's luck; 鷲憂雲 = a blue eagle in the cloud.

Karen
(f) Danish form of Katherine; (EGW) see Katherine

佳琳

Kana transcription: カレン／かれん

Purely phonetic transcription: 歌漣　華連　花蓮　佳恋　香練　賀簾　可憐

Purely denotative transcription: See Katherine

Phonetic & denotative transcription: 佳琳 = an excellent gem = hence "spotless purity"; 華琳 = a brilliant gem = hence "spotless purity."

Phonetic & eulogistic transcription: 嫁恋 = a bride in love; 香蓮 = a fragrant lotus; 華漣 = brilliant mild waves; 華恋 = a brilliant love; 可憐 = one who is amiable.

Attention-getting transcription: 嘩恋 = a noisy love; 鹿恋 = a deer which is in love; 誇恋 = a proud love.

Kate
(f) Pet form of Katherine (LDWG); see Katherine

蛍燈

Kana transcription: ケイト／けいと

Purely phonetic transcription: 佳威頭　恵徒　慶都　敬頭　桂杜　軽妬　慧兎

Purely denotative transcription: See Katherine

Phonetic & denotative transcription: 鏡鍍 = a plated mirror = "spotless purity"; 蛍燈 = a firefly's lamp = "spotless purity."

Phonetic & eulogistic transcription: 嫁偉登 = a bride who has become great; 華威騰 = one whose brilliance and dignity have increased; 快意人 = a person who has a pleasant intention; 敬頭 = a respected boss; 恵人 = a benevolent person; 慧頭 = a wise boss.

Attention-getting transcription: 怪猪頭 = a monstrous wild boar boss; 嫁猪途 = a wild boar's bride is on the way; 化偉杜 = a great ghost in the woods.

Kathy

(f) Pet form of Katherine (LDWG); see Katherine

Kana transcription: キャセイ／きゃせい

Purely phonetic transcription: 気屋背位　喜矢勢
貴野清　嬉夜盛　揮哉聖　輝耶誠　機也精

Purely denotative transcription: See Katherine

Phonetic & denotative transcription: 輝射星 = a brightly
shining star = hence "spotless purity."

Phonetic & eulogistic transcription: 貴家盛 = a prosperous noble
family; 嬉射妻 = a wife radiating joy; 輝野聖 = a shining holy
field; 喜夜聖 = a joyful holy night; 希家妻 = the lady of a
promising house.

Attention-getting transcription: 鬼射星 = a demon which shoots
stars; 亀野楼 = a tortoise living in the field.

Kay

(f) Greek, Latin, "pure"; "rejoicing" (ECS); also used as
a pet form of Katherine (EGW)

Kana transcription: ケイ／けい

Purely phonetic transcription: 佳位　嫁偉　華威
花慰　快意　敬　恵　慶　慧

Purely denotative transcription: 喜 = joy, *yorokobi*; 祝賀
= rejoicings, *shukuga*; 歓喜 = joy, *kanki*; 喜悦 = joy, *kietsu*; 欣喜
= *joy*, kinki; 愉悦 = rejoicing, *yuetsu*.

Phonetic & denotative transcription: 快慰 = a pleasant consolation =
hence "rejoicing"; 慶 = rejoicing.

Phonetic & eulogistic transcription: 嫁偉 = a great bride; 華威 =
one who is brilliant and dignified; 花慰 = a consoling flower; 快意
= a pleasant intention; 敬 = respect; 恵 = benevolence; 慶 =
rejoicing; 慧 = wisdom.

Attention-getting transcription: 怪猪 = a monstrous wild boar; 嫁
猪 = a wild boar's bride; 化偉 = a great ghost.

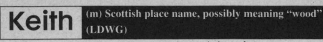

Keith

(m) Scottish place name, possibly meaning "wood" (LDWG)

Kana transcription: ケイス／けいす

Purely phonetic transcription: 嫁偉州　華威主　慧子 花慰守　快意素　佳寿　敬司　恵巣　慶蘇

Purely denotative transcription: 林 = a wood, *hayashi*; 森 = a wood, *mori*; 森林 = a wood, *shinrin*; 樹林 = a wood, *jurin*; 山 林 = a wood, *sanrin*.

Phonetic & denotative transcription: 桂州 = a state filled with Japanese Judas trees = hence a "wood."

Phonetic & eulogistic transcription: 慧偉寿 = one who is wise, great and long-living; 華威司 = a brilliant and dignified official; 花 施子 = a child who does flower arrangement; 快意主 = a manager with a pleasant intention; 敬司 = a respected official; 恵主 = a benevolent master; 慧子 = a wise child.

Attention-getting transcription: 怪猪巣 = a monstrous wild boar in the nest; 嫁猪守 = a wild boar which defends his bride; 化偉蘇 = a revived great ghost.

Ken

(m) Pet form of Kenneth (LDWG); see Kenneth

Kana transcription: ケン／けん

Purely phonetic transcription: 快員　佳音　華姻 賢　剣　研　健　絢　謙　牽　権　献　憲

Purely denotative transcription: See Kenneth

Phonetic & denotative transcription: 快胤 = a pleasant descendant = hence "handsome"; 佳員 = a handsome person = hence "handsome"; 絢 = "handsome"; 妍 = beautiful = hence "handsome."

Phonetic & eulogistic transcription: 快員 = a pleasant person; 佳音 = a beautiful sound; 華姻 = a brilliant marriage; 花蔭 = a shadow of a flower; 健 = a healthy person; 賢 = a wise person; 剣 = a sword.

Attention-getting transcription: 怪院 = a suspicious temple; 犬 = a dog; 拳 = a fist; 喧 = a quarrel; 険 = danger.

Kenneth
(m) Celtic, "good-looking, handsome" (GRS)

Kana transcription: ケネス／けねす

Purely phonetic transcription: 気音州　佳根巣
家襴寿　華値諏　毛子須

Purely denotative transcription: 美男 = handsome, *binan*;
美男子 = handsome, *binanshi*; 好男子 = handsome, *kodanshi*; 男
前 = handsome, *otokomae*; 玉人 = handsome, *gyokujin*.

Phonetic & denotative transcription: 佳寧子 = a handsome and
polite child = hence "handsome."

Phonetic & eulogistic transcription: 佳音子 = a beautiful sounding
child; 快寧主 = a pleasant and polite master; 慧根司 = an official
who is basically wise; 恵値主 = a master who sets benevolent
prices.

Attention-getting transcription: 毛根素 = one whose hair roots are
scarce; 化寧子 = a polite little ghost; 怪寧守 = a suspicious, but
polite guardian.

Kent
**(m) Place name, possibly meaning "rim, border"
(LDWG)**

Kana transcription: ケント／けんと

Purely phonetic transcription: 剣都　賢渡　犬登
件戸　県頭　検図　牽鍍　権妬　健徒　献兎

Purely denotative transcription: 縁 = rim, *fuchi*; 境 =
border, *sakai*; 境界 = border, *kyokai*; 国境 = border, *kokkyo*; 分界
= border, *bunkai*.

Phonetic & denotative transcription: 圏図 = a diagram of a sphere =
hence "rim, border."

Phonetic & eulogistic transcription: 剣徒 = a sword man; 拳徒 = a
boxer; 賢頭 = a wise boss; 健人 = a healthy person; 謙人 = a
modest man.

Attention-getting transcription: 犬頭 = the boss of dogs; 犬妬 = a
jealous dog; 倦頭 = a head which gets tired easily.

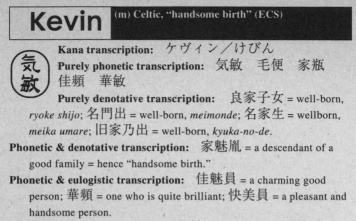

Kevin

(m) Celtic, "handsome birth" (ECS)

Kana transcription: ケヴィン／けびん

Purely phonetic transcription: 気敏　毛便　家瓶
佳頻　華敏

Purely denotative transcription: 良家子女 = well-born,
ryoke shijo; 名門出 = well-born, *meimonde*; 名家生 = wellborn,
meika umare; 旧家乃出 = well-born, *kyuka-no-de*.

Phonetic & denotative transcription: 家魅胤 = a descendant of a
good family = hence "handsome birth."

Phonetic & eulogistic transcription: 佳魅員 = a charming good
person; 華頻 = one who is quite brilliant; 快美員 = a pleasant and
handsome person.

Attention-getting transcription: 化敏 = a swift ghost; 毛貧 = one
who suffers from poor hair; 怪頻 = one who is often suspicious.

Kristen

(f) Latin, "Christian" (ECS); see Christina

Kana transcription: クリステン／くりすてん

Purely phonetic transcription: 苦裏巣店　救理数天
究麗諏点　倶悧須展　久哩寿典　栗州転

Purely denotative transcription: See Christina

Phonetic & denotative transcription: 基督員 = a
Christian = hence "one who carries Christ"; 基督縁 =
related to Christ = hence "one who carries Christ"; 基督援 = a
supporter of Christ = hence "one who carries Christ."

Phonetic & eulogistic transcription: 究理主天 = a heavenly lord
who seeks truth; 救痢子転 = one who saves a child injured by
tumbling down; 基督園 = Christ's garden = hence paradise; 基督
院 = Christ's house = hence a church.

Attention-getting transcription: 栗巣転 = a chestnut which rolls
down from the nest; 栗数十 = ten chestnuts.

Kyle

(m) Gaelic, "a strait"; "narrow piece of land" (LDWG)

誇居

Kana transcription: カイル／かいる

Purely phonetic transcription: 火位流　課委漏
華意瑠　花医琉　過威硫　歌偉留　貨畏劉
香居　界瑠　解要　会入

Purely denotative transcription: 海峡 = a strait, *kaikyo*; 海頸 = a strait, *kaikei*; 海門 = a strait, *kaimon*; 半島 = a peninsula, *hanto*; 地峡 = an isthmus, *kikyo*.

Phonetic & denotative transcription: 過萎留 = to remain in one place and wither = hence "a strait, narrow piece of land."

Phonetic & eulogistic transcription: 佳威留 = one who is good and dignified; 誇居 = a proud one; 華偉漏 = one who exudes brilliance and greatness; 香畏流 = one who exudes fragrance and solemnity.

Attention-getting transcription: 海流 = a sea current; 蚊囲留 = mosquitoes surrounding us; 鹿威留 = a dignified deer; 化偉留 = a great ghost.

Laura

(f) Feminine form of Laurence (HS); see Laurence

浪等

Kana transcription: ローラ／ろーら

Purely phonetic transcription: 路雨良　慮優等
露雄羅　浪等　朗裸　良羅

Purely denotative transcription: See Laurence

Phonetic & denotative transcription: 櫨優良 = an good and elegant wax tree = hence a "bay tree."

Phonetic & eulogistic transcription: 慮雄良 = one who is considerate and heroic; 露優蝸 = tender dew drops on a snail; 慮鶯蘿 = a considerate nightingale in the ivy.

Attention-getting transcription: 魯鴨蘿 = a stupid wild duck in the ivy; 狼追騾 = a wolf which chases a mule.

Brainteaser: 低騾 = a short mule. Note: "Lau-" (= low) = 低 in Japanese. Hence it is read "Laura."

Laurence
(m) Latin, "laurel"; "bay tree" (GRS)

霊木

Kana transcription: ローレンス／ろーれんす

Purely phonetic transcription: 路雨連州　朗錬須
老練諏　牢蓮簾　廊憐寿　浪漣須　郎恋数

Purely denotative transcription: 月桂樹 = laurel,
gekkeiju; 霊木 = a divine tree, *reiboku*; 優勝冠 = a victory crown,
yushokan.

Phonetic & denotative transcription: 櫨優連洲 = elegant wax trees
lined up around the sand bank = hence "bay tree."

Phonetic & eulogistic transcription: 老練主 = an expert manager;
朧恋守 = a guardian of love in the moonlight; 慮優恋司 = an
official who has a considerate and elegant love affair; 朗恋寿 = a
cheerful long-living love.

Attention-getting transcription: 狼恋巣 = a wolf which falls in love
in the nest; 鷺連主 = the master of the heron league; 魯恋司 = an
official's stupid love affair or a stupid official's love affair.

Lee
(m & f) English surname deriving from a place name,
"wood"; "clearing"; "meadow" (LDWG)

麗囲

Kana transcription: リー／りー

Purely phonetic transcription: 理医　離意　吏委
利偉　麗威　李畏　履移

Purely denotative transcription: 樹木 = a wood, *jumoku*;
林 = a wood, *hayashi*; 森 = a wood, *mori*; 森林 = a wood, *shinrin*;
空地 = clearing, *akichi*; 牧草地 = a meadow, *bokusochi*; 草地 = a
meadow, *kusachi*.

Phonetic & denotative transcription: 麗囲 = a beautiful "clearing."

Phonetic & eulogistic transcription: 梨囲 = a pear field; 利医 = a
clever doctor; 理威 = one who is wise and dignified; 礼医 = a
courteous doctor; 吏威 = a dignified official.

Attention-getting transcription: 鯉井 = a carp in the well; 狸偉 = a
great badger; 利猪 = a clever wild boar; 麗猪 = an elegant wild
boar.

Leo
(m) Greek, Latin, "lion" (EGW)

Kana transcription: レオ／れお

Purely phonetic transcription: 霊緒　礼夫　嶺尾　令雄　励御　鈴悪

Purely denotative transcription: 獅子 = a lion, *shishi*; 俊猊 = a lion, *shungei*; 獅子王 = lion king, *shishio*.

Phonetic & denotative transcription: 麗尾 = an elegant tail (of a lion) = hence a "lion"; 麗雄 = an elegant male = hence a "lion."

Phonetic & eulogistic transcription: 励夫 = an industrious husband; 怜雄 = a clever hero; 麗皇 = an elegant king.

Attention-getting transcription: 霊尾 = the tail of a ghost; 怜鴬 = a wise nightingale; 励鴨 = an industrious wild duck; 狸王 = the king of badgers; 霊悪 = a bad ghost.

Leonard
(m) Old German, compound of "lion" and "hardy, bold" (EGW)

Kana transcription: レナード／れなーど

Purely phonetic transcription: 霊名雅度　嶺那努　礼菜亜土　令奈阿奴　励菜亜怒

Purely denotative transcription: 大胆獅子 = a bold lion, *daitan shishi*; 強豪獣王 = the strong king of animals, *kyogo hyakuju*; 雄壮獅子王 = bold lion king, *yuso shishio*.

Phonetic & denotative transcription: 麗納雅怒 = one who roars elegantly with a beautiful finish = a "hardy lion."

Phonetic & eulogistic transcription: 麗名阿土 = a handsome person who is famous in Africa; 嶺菜雅怒 = one who roars elegantly in the mountains; 麗南留土 = a handsome person staying in the south.

Attention-getting transcription: 霊名雅怒 = a famous, elegant and angry ghost; 礼鳴努 = one who makes an effort to sing politely; 狸名雅洞 = a famous badger in an elegant cave.

Leslie

(f) From Leslie, "garden of hollies" (ECS)

Kana transcription: レスレー／れすれー
Purely phonetic transcription: 礼州礼　令巣令
麗寿麗　鈴須麗　嶺素霊　零数零　励諏令
Purely denotative transcription: 柊園庭 = a garden of
hollies, *hiragi entei*; 疼木庭園 = a garden of hollies, *hiragi
teien*; 砒裏蛄木林泉 = a garden of hollies, *toboku rinsen*.

Phonetic & denotative transcription: 麗杜領 = a beautiful forest
territory = hence close to a "garden of hollies."

Phonetic & eulogistic transcription: 礼主麗 = a courteous and
graceful master; 励司礼 = an official who makes an effort to be
courteous; 怜頭麗 = a clever and elegant boss.

Attention-getting transcription: 狸杜麗 = a badger in a beautiful
forest; 利頭霊 = a clever ghost.

Lillian

**(f) As now used, signifies "purity," but in its
original form it meant "heaven" (HS)**

Kana transcription: リリアン／りりあん
Purely phonetic transcription: 利里案　理璃案
里利安　裡離杏　吏離庵　麗里按　履哩案
Purely denotative transcription: 純潔 = purity, *junketsu*;
無垢 = purity, *muku* or 天 = heaven, *ten*; 極楽 = heaven/paradise,
gokuraku; 空 = heaven/sky, *sora*; 百合 = a lily, *yuri*.

Phonetic & denotative transcription: 離霊庵 = a vacation home for
the spirit = hence "heaven"; 離里安 = a far away peaceful place =
hence "heaven."

Phonetic & eulogistic transcription: 利麗安 = one who is clever,
elegant and peaceful; 理吏鞍 = an wise official in the saddle; 璃麗
庵 = an elegant gem at the vacation home.

Attention-getting transcription: 利狸暗 = a clever badger in the
dark; 理霊鞍 = an intelligent ghost in the saddle.

112

Linda
(f) Means "serpent," a symbol of wisdom (LDWG)

Kana transcription: リンダ／りんだ

Purely phonetic transcription: 林妥　輪柁　隣舵
厘舵　臨打　燐陀　麟妥

Purely denotative transcription: 蛇 = a serpent, *hebi*; 棟蛇 = a serpent, *toda* or 賢明 = wisdom, *kenmei*; 知恵 = wisdom, *chie*; 知識 = wisdom, *chie*.

Phonetic & denotative transcription: 林蛇 = a serpent in the forest or forest serpent = hence a "serpent"; 輪蛇 = a coiled serpent = hence a "serpent."

Phonetic & eulogistic transcription: 利運娜 = a lucky beauty; 麗雲大 = a large elegant cloud; 倫娜 = an ethical beauty; 淋娜 = a lonely beauty; 琳大 = a great gem; 鈴打 = a bell striker.

Attention-getting transcription: 隣娜 = a beauty next door; 鈴駄 = a worthless bell; 淋惰 = one who is lonely and lazy.

Lisa
(f) Hebrew, "oath of God" (ECS); pet form of Elizabeth (LDWG), see Elizabeth

Kana transcription: リーザ／りーざ

Purely phonetic transcription: 利偉座　理意坐
麗威座　璃位座　履慰挫

Purely denotative transcription: See Elizabeth

Phonetic & denotative transcription: 霊意座 = the intention of the spirit remains = hence "oath of God"; 理叡座 = providence which remains = hence "oath of God"; 離意挫 = the intention to avoid failures = hence "oath of God."

Phonetic & eulogistic transcription: 理偉座 = great intelligence at rest; 利威座 = cleverness and dignity that remain; 麗医座 = an elegant female doctor who is seated; 璃威坐 = a gem that sits with dignity; 霊畏座 = a spirit sitting respectfully.

Attention-getting transcription: 狸医坐 = a badger doctor who is sitting; 鯉井坐 = a carp which remains in the well; 利施挫 = one who fails in making profits.

Lori

(f) Spanish, Germanic, "the laurel"; "symbol of victory"; pet form of Laura (ECS)

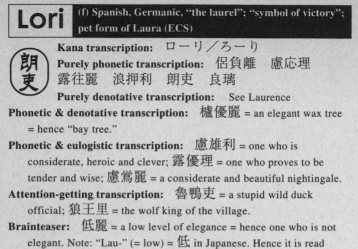

Kana transcription: ローリ／ろーり

Purely phonetic transcription: 侶負離　慮応理　露往麗　浪押利　朗吏　良璃

Purely denotative transcription: See Laurence

Phonetic & denotative transcription: 櫨優麗 = an elegant wax tree = hence "bay tree."

Phonetic & eulogistic transcription: 慮雄利 = one who is considerate, heroic and clever; 露優理 = one who proves to be tender and wise; 慮嘗麗 = a considerate and beautiful nightingale.

Attention-getting transcription: 魯鴨吏 = a stupid wild duck official; 狼王里 = the wolf king of the village.

Brainteaser: 低麗 = a low level of elegance = hence one who is not elegant. Note: "Lau-" (= low) = 低 in Japanese. Hence it is read "Lori."

Lorraine

(f) French, Lorraine province; associated with Joan of Arc, born in Lorraine (LDWG)

Kana transcription: ロレーン／ろれーん

Purely phonetic transcription: 路連　炉錬　露恋　呂漣　蕗憐　魯蓮　鷺簾

Purely denotative transcription: 仏蘭西地方名 = a French province, *furansuchihomei*.

Phonetic & denotative transcription: not available

Phonetic & eulogistic transcription: 老練 = a veteran; 慮礼員 = a considerate and courteous person; 朗怜胤 = a cheerful and wise descendant; 旅励員 = an industrious traveller.

Attention-getting transcription: 魯連 = a league of fools; 鷺嶺隠 = a snowy heron hiding on the ridge; 老霊姻 = an old ghost which marries.

Brainteaser: 露雨 = a dew-like rain; 慮雨 = a considerate rain; 朗雨 = a cheerful rain. Note: "-raine" (= rain) = 雨 in Japanese. Hence all these are read "Lorraine."

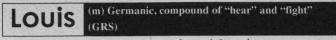

Louis (m) Germanic, compound of "hear" and "fight" (GRS)

Kana transcription: ルイス／るいす

Purely phonetic transcription: 瑠委諏　留畏数　累主　硫移州　琉異素　類州　塁巣　涙諏　留椅子

Purely denotative transcription: 聞戦 = hear and fight, *bunsen*; 聞響戦闘 = hear and fight, *bunkyo sento*; 耳聞交戦 = hear and fight, *jibun kosen*.

Phonetic & denotative transcription: 留威守 = a feudal governor who always keeps an imposing posture in preparation for a fight = hence "fight"; 流移吸 = to take in what is rumored = hence to "hear"; 留施守 = to stay prepared for defense = hence "fight."

Phonetic & eulogistic transcription: 漏威崇 = one who exudes dignity and nobility; 留偉司 = an great official; 流威主 = a master who exudes dignity and nobility; 留医寿 = a long-living doctor.

Attention-getting transcription: 流移司 = a vagabond official; 流椅子 = a chair floating downstream; 漏囲雛 = a fledgling which falls out of the nest; 留猪寿 = a long-living wild boar.

Louise (f) French feminine form of Louis (GRS); see Louis

Kana transcription: ルイーズ／るいーず

Purely phonetic transcription: 瑠委畏頭　留畏意杜　硫移偉徒　琉施異逗　流威図　瑠偉頭　留意逗　類図　塁徒　涙杜　累途

Purely denotative transcription: See Louis

Phonetic & denotative transcription: 留威偉頭 = a great head who keeps an imposing posture in preparation for a fight = hence "fight"; 流移受 = to receive what is rumored = hence to "hear."

Phonetic & eulogistic transcription: 留偉位徒 = a follower retaining great rank = a top-ranking bright pupil; 留医徒 = one who remains a medical student; 瑠偉杜 = a great gem in the forest.

Attention-getting transcription: 流移豆 = a bean floating downstream; 留猪頭 = one which remains a wild boar boss.

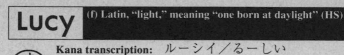

LUCY

(f) Latin, "light," meaning "one born at daylight" (HS)

Kana transcription: ルーシイ／るーしい

Purely phonetic transcription: 留使意　瑠視畏
流紙偉　琉氏畏　硫詩威

Purely denotative transcription: 光 = light, *hikari*; 光明 = light, *komyo*; 光輝 = light, *koki*; 光華 = light, *koka*; 光燭 = light, *koshoku*.

Phonetic & denotative transcription: 流星 = a falling star = hence "light"; 流宇差移 = something which moves in from the cosmos to light up = hence "light"; 琉紫偉 = a great purple gem = hence "shining."

Phonetic & eulogistic transcription: 漏示威 = one who shows dignity; 流優姿医 = a doctor whose has a graceful body line; 流詩移 = a wandering poet.

Attention-getting transcription: 流芋食猪 = a wild boar which eats a potato floating in the water; 婁憂姉移 = an unstable elder sister who is often blue; 留雨脂猪 = a fat wild boar in the rain.

Luke

(m) Greek, "wolf" or from place name "Lucania," a district in Southern Italy (LDWG)

Kana transcription: ルク／るく

Purely phonetic transcription: 瑠究　流苦　琉供
屡功

Purely denotative transcription: 伊太利地方名 = an Italian district, *itaria chiho-mei* or 狼 = a wolf, *okami*.

Phonetic & denotative transcription: 流狗 = a nomad dog = hence a "wolf"; 婁狗 = often a dog = hence "a wolf."

Phonetic & eulogistic transcription: 琉久 = an eternal gem; 流公 = a wandering duke; 瑠空 = a gem-like sky = hence the blue sky; 婁救 = one who often saves; 流香 = one who gives off a fragrance.

Attention-getting transcription: 流狗 = a wandering dog; 留苦 = one who is suffering from pain; 漏駒 = a urinating horse.

Lynn
(f) Pet form of Linda (LDWG); see Linda

Kana transcription: リン／りん

Purely phonetic transcription: 麗姻　理員　璃院
鈴　倫　淋　琳

Purely denotative transcription: See Linda

Phonetic & denotative transcription: 鱗 = something that has scales
= hence a "serpent."

Phonetic & eulogistic transcription: 吏員 = an official; 麗音 = one
who has an elegant voice; 利員 = a clever person; 鈴 = a bell; 倫 =
a chaste person.

Attention-getting transcription: 狸姻 = a badger's marriage; 離飲 =
one who stops drinking; 淋 = a lonely person.

Malcolm
**(m) Gaelic, "servant or disciple of Columb,"
a popular Scottish name (EGW)**

Kana transcription: マルコム／まるこむ

Purely phonetic transcription: 魔流固務　摩留誇無
麻瑠庫霧　馬留顧夢　真琉鼓武　丸込　円混
円湖舞

Purely denotative transcription: 個留運武召使 = servant of
Columb, *korunbu meshitsukai* or 聖人弟子 = disciple of a saint,
seijin deshi.

Phonetic & denotative transcription: 真留貢務 = one who sincerely
offers services (to his master) = hence a "servant"; 間留講務 = one
who is busy listening to the (master's) lectures and giving services =
hence a "disciple."

Phonetic & eulogistic transcription: 磨琉工務 = a gem polisher; 磨
留功夢 = one who improves himself dreaming of a success; 真留
誇武 = a really proud samurai; 真瑠護務 = one in charge of
defending authentic gems.

Attention-getting transcription: 魔留湖霧 = a demon which lives in
a foggy lake; 馬婁誇舞 = a horse which frequently boasts of its
dance; 馬流狐夢 = a fox which dreams of a horse is floating
downstream.

117

Manuel (m) Hebrew, "God is with us" (ECS)

Kana transcription: マヌエル／まぬえる

Purely phonetic transcription: 磨怒慧留　真奴衛瑠
馬怒恵琉　麻怒江流

Purely denotative transcription: 神民一体 = God and
people in one body, *jinmin ittai*; 神民一緒 = God and people
together, *jinmin issho*; 神民一身 = God and people in one
body, *jinmin isshin*.

Phonetic & denotative transcription: 間怒恵留 = to be between
(God's) anger and benevolence = hence "God is with us"; 真怒恵
留 = one who remains true to (God) whether he is angry or
benevolent = hence "God is with us."

Phonetic & eulogistic transcription: 真怒兄留 = a really angry
elder brother; 真奴衛留 = one who seriously defends his people;
真縫衣瑠 = one who sews a gem onto a dress.

Attention-getting transcription: 魔怒永留 = an eternally angry
demon; 魔能泳流 = a demon which is capable of swimming.

Mark (m) Latin, "of Mars"; "god of war" (ECS)

Kana transcription: マーク／まーく

Purely phonetic transcription: 磨亜句　真阿玖
馬雅久　魔亜究　間阿駈

Purely denotative transcription: 軍神 = a god of war,
gunshin; 武神 = a god of war, *bushin*; 戦神 = war god, *ikusa-gami*.

Phonetic & denotative transcription: 真雅攻守 = a truly elegant
guardian who is attacking = hence "god of war"; 真雅抗守 = a
truly elegant guardian who is defending = hence "god of war."

Phonetic & eulogistic transcription: 真雅家主 = a really elegant
house master; 磨雅誇司 = a proud official who practices elegance;
間婀誇主 = a master who is proud of being among beauties.

Attention-getting transcription: 馬雅嫁取 = a horse which takes an
elegant bride; 磨雅鹿守 = a deer keeper who practices beautifully.

Margaret
(f) Persian, "pearl" or "child of light" (HS)

Kana transcription: マーガレット／まーがれっと

Purely phonetic transcription: 磨亜雅令戸
真阿賀霊妬　馬雅我嶺頭　魔亜伽励杜

Purely denotative transcription: 真珠 = a pearl, *shinju*; 貝珠 = a pearl, *baishu*; 明珠 = a pearl, *meishu*; 明月珠 = a pearl, *meigetsushu*; 阿古屋珠 = a pearl, *akoya dama* or 光子 = light child, *mitsuko*.

Phonetic & denotative transcription: 真雅賀麗瞳 = a really elegant, happy and beautiful pupil = hence a "pearl"; 真雅賀麗鍍 = really elegant, happy and beautiful plating = hence a "pearl."

Phonetic & eulogistic transcription: 磨婀雅礼度 = a beauty who often practices elegance and courtesy; 真婀雅怜努 = a real beauty who tries to be elegant and wise; 馬婀駕励努 = a beauty who tries to ride on a horse.

Attention-getting transcription: 馬唖雅励度 = a horse which often tries to laugh elegantly and politely; 魔蛙餓裂頭 = a demon who breaks the head of a hungry frog.

Marian
(f) Diminutive of Mary (EGW); see Mary

Kana transcription: マリアン／まりあん

Purely phonetic transcription: 真理鞍　万里庵
茉利安　磨麗按　真理杏

Purely denotative transcription: See Mary

Phonetic & denotative transcription: 真離行 = to really leave (one's family/friends) = hence "bitterness."

Phonetic & eulogistic transcription: 真麗安 = one who is really elegant and peaceful; 磨理安 = one who improves her intelligence and stability; 魔理譜 = one who is capable of magical and logical memorization; 真利按 = one who thinks really cleverly.

Attention-getting transcription: 馬理安 = a wise and peaceful horse; 魔狸暗 = a devilish badger in the dark.

Marilyn

(f) Compound of Mary and Lynn (GRS); see Mary and Lynn

Kana transcription: マリリン／まりりん

Purely phonetic transcription: 真理麗姻　万里理員
茉利璃院　磨麗倫　真理淋　磨璃琳　鞠鈴

Purely denotative transcription: See Mary and Lynn/Linda

Phonetic & denotative transcription: 真離鱗 = something that completely sheds its scales = hence a "serpent."

Phonetic & eulogistic transcription: 真麗璃引 = one who wears really beautiful gems; 真利麗姻 = a truly clever and beautiful marriage; 真麗利員 = a really beautiful and clever person; 魔利鈴 = a clever magic bell; 真麗淋 = one who is very graceful and lonely.

Attention-getting transcription: 馬利狸姻 = a wise horse which marries a badger; 真狸離飲 = a badger which really stops drinking.

Mario

(m) Hebrew, Latin, "bitterness"; "of Mars, god of war" (ECS)

Kana transcription: マリオ／まりお

Purely phonetic transcription: 真理雄　万里王
茉利桜　磨麗尾　真理皇

Purely denotative transcription: 辛苦 = bitterness, *shinku*; 辛酸 = bitterness, *shinsan*; 辛気 = bitterness, *shinki*; 苦労 = bitterness, *kuro*; 大儀 = bitterness, *kuro* or 軍神 = a god of war, *gunshin*; 武神 = a god of war, *bushin*; 戦神 = a god of war, *ikusagami*.

Phonetic & denotative transcription: 真離夫 = a husband who has been really divorced = hence "bitterness" and 馬利雄 = a clever hero on a horse = hence a "god of war."

Phonetic & eulogistic transcription: 真麗夫 = a truly handsome husband; 真利雄 = a truly clever hero; 真吏雄 = a truly heroic official; 真理王 = a truly intelligent king.

Attention-getting transcription: 馬理雄 = a wise and heroic horse.

Marjorie

(f) French popular form of Margaret (EGW); see Margaret

Kana transcription: マージョリー／まーじょりー

Purely phonetic transcription: 磨雅女利医
真阿助理畏　馬雅序麗偉　魔亜情麗

Purely denotative transcription: See Margaret

Phonetic & denotative transcription: 真雅女麗 = a very elegant, beautiful woman = hence a "pearl"; 真雅浄麗 = a thing which is truly elegant, pure and beautiful = hence a "pearl."

Phonetic & eulogistic transcription: 磨女利威 = a woman who improves her cleverness and dignity; 真助吏偉 = a great official who extends real help; 真情理畏 = one who is really sympathetic, wise and solemn.

Attention-getting transcription: 磨雅杖霊 = the ghost which polishes its elegant stick; 馬唖女狸 = a horse which laughs at a female badger; 魔蛙助齢 = a devilish frog which helps the old.

Martha

(f) Aramaic, "lady or mistress of the house" (LDWG)

Kana transcription: マーサ／まーさ

Purely phonetic transcription: 間阿紗　磨亜瑳
真阿嵯　馬雅作　魔亜鎖　間阿査　磨亜佐

Purely denotative transcription: 主婦 = a housewife, *shufu*; 家婦 = a housewife, *kafu*; 家刀自 = a housewife, *ietoji*; 家庭婦人 = a housewife, *katei fujin*.

Phonetic & denotative transcription: 間雅磋 = one who polishes rooms beautifully = hence "lady or mistress of the house."

Phonetic & eulogistic transcription: 馬雅瑳 = one who polishes a horse cleanly = hence a "horse trainer"; 真雅紗 = a really elegant cloth.

Attention-getting transcription: 魔婀詐 = a demon which deceives a beauty; 馬唖鎖 = a horse which laughs at the chain; 馬雅茶 = a horse which drinks elegant tea.

Martin
(m) Latin, "of Mars"; "god of war" (GRS)

Kana transcription: マーテイン／まーてぃん

Purely phonetic transcription: 魔阿手員　磨亜手韻　真阿手院　馬雅手蔭　魔亜手引　間阿手印

Purely denotative transcription: 軍神 = a god of war, *gunshin*; 武神 = a god of war, *bushin*; 戦神 = war god, *ikusa-gami*.

Phonetic & denotative transcription: 真雅填 = to calm or terminate war very elegantly = hence "god of war."

Phonetic & eulogistic transcription: 真雅帝胤 = a really elegant royal descendant; 磨雅貞員 = a person who practices elegance and constancy; 馬雅帝引 = an emperor who leads an elegant horse.

Attention-getting transcription: 馬雅転 = a horse which falls elegantly; 魔手隠 = a demon which hides hands.

Brainteaser: 馬拾 = ten horses; 魔拾 = ten demons. Note: "-tin" (= ten) = 拾 in Japanese. Hence both are read "Martin".

Mary
(f) Hebrew, "bitterness" (HS)

Kana transcription: メアリー／めありー

Purely phonetic transcription: 芽阿利意　雌亜麗　女雅利異　目阿璃位　馬雅理偉　奴亜梨畏

Purely denotative transcription: 辛苦 = bitterness, *shinku*; 辛酸 = bitterness, *shinsan*; 辛気 = bitterness, *shinki*; 苦労 = bitterness, *kuro*; 大儀 = bitterness, *kuro*.

Phonetic & denotative transcription: 芽会冷 = young buds which meet cold weather = hence "bitterness"; 女逢令 = a woman who comes across severe orders = hence "bitterness"; 雌遭霊 = a woman who encounters a ghost = hence "bitterness."

Phonetic & eulogistic transcription: 芽婀麗 = an graceful young beauty; 明雅礼 = one who is bright, elegant and courteous; 名婀礼偉 = a great beauty who is famous and courteous.

Attention-getting transcription: 目蛙麗 = a frog which has charming eyes; 雌蟻偉 = a great female ant; 雌蛙離猪 = a female frog which divorces a wild boar.

Matthew
(m) Hebrew, "gift of Jehovah" (EGW)

Kana transcription: マシュー／ましゅう

Purely phonetic transcription: 摩秀　間周　磨週
真修　魔蹴　麻酬　馬集

Purely denotative transcription: 神進物 = gift of God,
kami shinmotsu; 神贈品 = gift of God, *shin zohin*; 主恵物 = gift
of the Lord, *shu keibutsu*; 主信物 = gift of the Lord, *shu shinmotsu*.

Phonetic & denotative transcription: 真主右 = the true Lord gives
us help = hence "gift of Jehovah"; 真主雨 = the true Lord gives rain
= hence "gift of Jehovah"; 真主宇 = the true Lord gives the
universe = hence "gift of Jehovah."

Phonetic & eulogistic transcription: 真詩雄 = a true heroic poet; 真
師優 = a very tender teacher; 馬侍勇 = a brave knight; 真司裕 =
a really well-off official.

Attention-getting transcription: 馬愁 = a melancholy horse; 馬讐 =
a revenging horse; 魔鷲 = a devilish eagle; 馬蹴 = a kicking horse.

Brainteaser: 馬靴 = horse shoes; 魔靴 = a magic shoes. Note:
"-tthew" (=shoe) = 靴 in Japanese. Hence both are read "Matthew."

Maureen
**(f) Irish diminutive of Mary (GRS); see
Mary**

Kana transcription: モーリーン／もーりーん

Purely phonetic transcription: 毛利院　望理員
網里韻　耗璃引　蒙琳　忙淋

Purely denotative transcription: See Mary

Phonetic & denotative transcription: 猛冷姻 = a terribly cold
marriage = "bitterness"; 母圧離縁 = a mother obliged to be
divorced = "bitterness"; 忙履姻 = too busy to get married =
"bitterness."

Phonetic & eulogistic transcription: 最優理員 = the wisest and
most graceful person; 望倫 = one who seeks to be ethical; 母優倫
= a tender and ethical mother; 最大琳 = the largest gem.

Attention-getting transcription: 猛狸飲 = a badger which drinks
heavily; 猛淋 = one who is terribly lonely.

Maurice

(m) Latin, "a Moor" (RGS)

耗
璃
諏

Kana transcription: モーリス／もーりす

Purely phonetic transcription: 毛利州　猛理巣
孟里酸　耗璃諏　蒙哩須　忙梨寿　望履素
網裡司　冒吏主

Purely denotative transcription: 北阿弗利加人 = A
north-African, *kita-afurika-jin*.

Phonetic & denotative transcription: 猛阿里子 = a courageous
child of an African village = hence "a Moor."

Phonetic & eulogistic transcription: 最優理主 = the most graceful
and wise master; 望理司 = an official who seeks to be intelligent;
猛理守 = a brave and wise guardian; 最大璃周 = the gem of the
largest sphere = hence the largest gem.

Attention-getting transcription: 猛栗鼠 = a ferocious squirrel; 毛
離主 = a hair-losing master; 忙励子 = a busy and industrious
child; 猛里主 = a violent village mayor.

Megan

(f) Welsh pet form of Margaret (LDWG); see
Margaret

女
願

Kana transcription: メガン／めがん

Purely phonetic transcription: 女雅運　芽臥温
馬顔　雌頑　芽願　女巌

Purely denotative transcription: See Margaret

Phonetic & denotative transcription: 目丸 = a round eyeball = hence
a "pearl"; 女願 = what all women want = hence a "pearl."

Phonetic & eulogistic transcription: 女雅運 = a woman who has an
elegant luck; 目雅員 = a person who has elegant eyes; 女頑 = an
industrious woman.

Attention-getting transcription: 雌雁 = a female wild goose; 馬願 =
a demanding horse; 目癌 = one who suffers from eye cancer.

Melanie

Kana transcription: メラニー／めらにー

Purely phonetic transcription: 芽等尼威　目羅爾偉　叺螺仁位　女等児意　馬良荷移　雌羅丹畏

Purely denotative transcription: 浅黒 = dark, *asaguro*; 色黒 = black-colored, *iroguro*; 膚黒 = black-colored skin, *hadaguro*; 黒人 = a black person, *kokujin*.

Phonetic & denotative transcription: 名黎児為 = a child known for its black skin = hence "black."

Phonetic & eulogistic transcription: 名良尼 = a good nun who is famous; 名医裸児 = a famous doctor who keeps kids naked; 女医良仁 = a good and benevolent female doctor; 目威良尼 = a good nun who has dignified eyes.

Attention-getting transcription: 馬等尼囲 = a nun surrounded by horses; 雌騾荷猪 = a mule which carries a wild boar; 女裸児井 = a naked little girl in the well.

Melissa

Kana transcription: メリッサ／めりっさ

Purely phonetic transcription: 芽里差　目理査　雌利嵯　馬璃紗　女麗唆

Purely denotative transcription: 蜜蜂 = a honeybee, *mitsubachi*; 羅叉 = a bee, *rasa*; 遊蜂 = a bee, *yuho*; 金翼使 = a bee, *kin-yokushi*.

Phonetic & denotative transcription: 魅羅叉 = a charming bee = a "honeybee"; 美羅叉 = a beautiful bee = a "honeybee."

Phonetic & eulogistic transcription: 魅麗作 = one who has charming and graceful manners; 眼麗差 = one who has graceful eyes; 女麗紗 = a woman in elegant clothes; 雌吏査 = a female official inspector.

Attention-getting transcription: 芽離砂 = a sprout which shouts out of the sand; 雌狸嗟 = a sighing female badger.

Michael
(m) Hebrew, "Who is like God?"; one of the archangels (EGW)

Kana transcription: マイケル／まいける
Purely phonetic transcription: 間委家瑠　魔医毛留
枚蹴裏蕚　毎気硫　舞袈瑠　米蹴　妹佳留
Purely denotative transcription: 大天使 = an archangel, *dai-tenshi*; 天使長 = an archangel, *tenshi-cho*.

Phonetic & denotative transcription: 舞来 = to come dancing in the air = hence the archangel; 媒希流 = one who mediates to scatter (to announce) hope (to Maria) = hence the "archangel."

Phonetic & eulogistic transcription: 真偉快留 = a great person who is really pleasant; 舞華流 = one who dances brilliantly; 真威佳留 = a good person who is really dignified; 磨違華瑠 = a gem which has been polished so brilliantly it looks like a different gem.

Attention-getting transcription: 魔猪蹴 = a demon who kicks a wild boar; 馬慰怪婁 = a horse which consoles a monster; 磨猪毛流 = one who polishes a wild boar's hair; 舞蹴 = one who kicks to dance = a can-can dancer; 魔威蹴 = one who kicks a horrifying demon.

Michelle
(f) French feminine form of Michael (GRS); see Michael

Kana transcription: ミッシル／みっしる
Purely phonetic transcription: 美姿得　御師留
魅姉瑠　魅司流　眉詩獲
Purely denotative transcription: See Michael
Phonetic & denotative transcription: 魅姿留 = a charming figure = hence "worthy of admiration"; 美詩流 = a beautifully flowing poem = hence "worthy of admiration"; 深識 = profound learning = hence "worthy of admiration."

Phonetic & eulogistic transcription: 美子瑠 = a beautiful gem-like child; 魅司留 = a handsome official; 御侍留 = a samurai; 魅知 = a charming and learned person.

Attention-getting transcription: 美獅流 = a beautiful lioness floating downstream; 美汁 = a delicious soup; 微知 = one who has little knowledge; 密知 = one who knows the secret.

Mick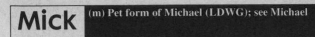

(m) Pet form of Michael (LDWG); see Michael

Kana transcription: ミック／みっく

Purely phonetic transcription: 美究　御公　魅功
実久　眉玖　味究

Purely denotative transcription: See Michael

Phonetic & denotative transcription: 魅躯 = a charming body = hence "worthy of admiration"; 美句 = a beautiful verse = hence "worthy of admiration"; 美久 = eternal beauty = hence "worthy of admiration."

Phonetic & eulogistic transcription: 美公 = a handsome duke; 深究 = a great scholar; 魅駒 = a charming horse; 実功 = one who has real merits.

Attention-getting transcription: 身苦 = one who has an ailing body; 魅狗 = a charming dog; 微功 = one who has few merits; 密究 = one who studies secretly.

Monica

(f) It is generally supposed to signify "alone" or "dwelling alone" (HS)

Kana transcription: モニカ／もにか

Purely phonetic transcription: 藻弐香　模荷価
最丹嘉　莫爾賀　摸児華　茂尼佳　裳仁加

Purely denotative transcription: 単独 = alone, *tandoku*; 孤独 = alone, *kodoku*; 孤身 = alone, *koshin*; 単孤 = alone, *tanko* or 単独居住 = dwelling alone, *tandoku kyoju*; 単身生活 = dwelling alone, *tanshin seikatsu*.

Phonetic & denotative transcription: 莫児嫁 = a childless bride = hence "alone"; 姥尼家 = an old nun's house = "dwelling alone."

Phonetic & eulogistic transcription: 模尼誇 = a proud model nun; 最仁嫁 = the most benevolent bride; 母仁佳 = a benevolent and good mother; 最尼華 = the most brilliant nun; 茂尼花 = a nun among the growing flowers.

Attention-getting transcription: 最児嫁 = the youngest bride; 猛尼暇 = a tough nun who has much time; 毛丹嫁 = a red-haired bride.

Morgan

(m) Welsh, compound of "sea" and "dweller" (RGS)

嬪御

Kana transcription: モーガン／もーがん

Purely phonetic transcription: 猛眼　毛雁　望含　忙顔　蒙丸　耗玩　孟巌

Purely denotative transcription: 海住人 = sea dweller, *umi-junin*; 海洋民 = sea dweller, *kaiyo-min*; 大洋住民 = sea dweller, *taiyo-jumin*; 蒼海居住者 = sea dweller, *sokai-kyojusha*.

Phonetic & denotative transcription: 網岸 = fish nets on the shore = hence "sea"; 望岸 = viewing the shore = hence a "sea dweller"; 忙岸 = busy shores = hence "sea"; 網玩 = fish nets used as toys = hence "sea" and "sea dweller."

Phonetic & eulogistic transcription: 猛巌 = one who is violent and stern; 望巌 = one who tries to be stern; 最雄駕運 = the greatest hero who rides on luck; 模雅員 = an elegant model person.

Attention-getting transcription: 孟眼 = large eyes; 猛顔 = a terrifying face; 忙雁 = a busy wild goose; 毛顔 = a hairy face.

Morton

(m) Common English place name, "village on a moor" (LDWG)

網嶼

Kana transcription: モートン／もーとん

Purely phonetic transcription: 網嶼　猛盾　帽惇　毛敦　望屯　忙沌　蒙遁　耗豚　孟鈍

Purely denotative transcription: 荒地村 = a village on a moor, *arechi-mura*; 荒野村落 = a village on a moor, *koya-sonraku*; 沼沢地部落 = a village on a moor, *numasawachi-buraku*.

Phonetic & denotative transcription: 莫芋站 = a village where even potatoes do not exist = hence "village on a moor."

Phonetic & eulogistic transcription: 模王敦 = a sincere model king; 最旺呑 = the most active drinker; 猛頭運 = a lucky, but violent boss.

Attention-getting transcription: 忙豚 = a busy pig; 猛呑 = a heavy drinker; 猛鈍 = one who is extremely dull.

Nancy

(f) Originally a pet form of Ann or Anne (LDWG); see Ann

難止

Kana transcription: ナンシー／なんしー

Purely phonetic transcription: 菜雅雲詩意　那安姿偉 楠枝威　南指医　難止位

Purely denotative transcription: See Ann

Phonetic & denotative transcription: 難止意 = the will to relieve trouble = hence "mercy."

Phonetic & eulogistic transcription: 娜運示 = a beauty who displays good luck; 菜雲施尉 = a flower under a cloud that consoles us; 南 指移 = one who moves towards the south; 男示慰 = one who shows consolation to a man; 軟姉威 = a soft dignified elder sister.

Attention-getting transcription: 難脂医 = a doctor troubled by fat; 難姉移 = an elder sister who gets into trouble; 南獅葦 = a southern lion in the reeds.

Neil

(m) Irish, "warrior"; "champion" (GRS)

荷射

Kana transcription: ニール／にーる

Purely phonetic transcription: 荷医漏　弐委留 荷意瑠　仁位硫　児威流　爾偉瑠　尼畏留

Purely denotative transcription: 武人 = a warrior, *bujin*; 兵士 = a warrior, *heishi*; 戦士 = a warrior, *senshi*; 猛者 = a warrior, *mosa* or 優勝者 = a champion, *yushosha*; 戦士 = a champion, *senshi*; 闘士 = a champion, *toshi*.

Phonetic & denotative transcription: 荷夷流 = one in charge of conquering barbarians = hence a "warrior"; 荷射 = one who is in charge of shooting = hence a "warrior."

Phonetic & eulogistic transcription: 仁威婁 = one who is often benevolent and dignified; 児畏留 = a solemn child; 仁医留 = a benevolent doctor; 新位留 = one in a new position.

Attention-getting transcription: 児猪留 = a wild boar child; 丹猪 流 = a wild red boar floating downstream; 新入 = a newcomer.

Nelson

(m) A surname, "son of Neil," used as a first name (LDWG)

Kana transcription: ネルソン／ねるそん

Purely phonetic transcription: 値留孫　襧瑠遜　根琉尊　音流村　練損　寝樽

Purely denotative transcription: 武人乃子 = a son of a warrior, *bujin-no-ko*; 兵士息子 = a son of a warrior, *heishi-musuko*; 戦士子息 = a son of the warrior, *senshi-shisoku* or 戦士子息 = a champion, *senshi-shisoku*; 闘士息子 = a son of the champion, *toshi-musuko*.

Phonetic & denotative transcription: 荷夷流残 = the descendant of the one in charge of driving out barbarians = a "son of warrior"; 子留争員 = a son of a fighter = a "son of warrior."

Phonetic & eulogistic transcription: 値入尊 = one who respects prices = a merchant; 寧留孫 = a polite grandson; 音映流存 = one who directs the flow of sound and images = a film director.

Attention-getting transcription: 寝孫 = a sleeping grandson; 練鱒 = a trout trainer; 寝樽 = one who sleeps in a barrel.

Nicholas

(m) Latin, Greek, compound of "victory" and "the people" (EGW)

Kana transcription: ニコラス／にこらす

Purely phonetic transcription: 弐瑚等巣　而護良州　荷誇螺寿　仁雇良須　児子等諏　爾醐羅素

Purely denotative transcription: 勝民 = victory and the people, *shomin*; 勝利人民 = victory and the people, *shori jinmin*; 戦勝民族 = victory and the people, *sensho minzoku*.

Phonetic & denotative transcription: 荷抗等守 = in charge of fighting back to defend people = hence "victory" and "people."

Phonetic & eulogistic transcription: 仁護等主 = a benevolent lord who defends people; 児誇良素 = a child who is proud, good and honest.

Attention-getting transcription: 丹狐良子 = a good red fox cub; 児好騾守 = a child who likes a mule and protects it.

Nick

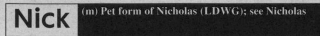

(m) Pet form of Nicholas (LDWG); see Nicholas

Kana transcription: ニック／にっく

Purely phonetic transcription: 仁公　児駒　弐久
荷究　爾功　尼救　丹玖

Purely denotative transcription: See Nicholas

Phonetic & denotative transcription: 仁救 = to save with benevolence = hence "victory" and "people."

Phonetic & eulogistic transcription: 日駆 = the sun driver = hence Apollo and Helios (Greek and Roman mythology); 仁究 = one who seeks benevolence; 尼救 = one who saves a nun; 児駈 = a running child; 荷玖 = a load of gems; 日空 = the sun in the sky or Japan Airlines.

Attention-getting transcription: 丹駒 = a red horse; 日喰 = one who eats the sun; 丹空 = the red sky; 荷苦 = one who carries pain/trouble; 日苦 = the sun is in trouble or one who suffers daily pain.

Nicky

(f) Feminine form of Nicholas (LDWG); see Nicholas

Kana transcription: ニッキイ／にっきい

Purely phonetic transcription: 仁騎偉　児輝畏
弐嬉慰　荷喜衣　丹輝威

Purely denotative transcription: See Nicholas

Phonetic & denotative transcription: 仁騎偉 = a great benevolent knight = hence "victory" and "people"; 荷揮慰 = one in charge of commanding and consoling = hence "victory" and "people."

Phonetic & eulogistic transcription: 日輝偉 = the great shining sun; 仁揮位 = a benevolent person who is in a commanding position; 児貴衣 = a child in noble clothes; 荷輝畏 = a precious shining cargo.

Attention-getting transcription: 丹亀 = a red tortoise; 日飢移 = the hungry sun; 丹鬼異 = a strange red devil; 荷危威 = a horrifyingly dangerous load.

Brainteaser: 日鍵 = the key to open the sun; 荷鍵 = the key to open the luggage. Note: "ky" (= key) = 鍵 in Japanese. Hence both are read "Nicky."

Norma
(f) Latin, "pattern"; "model" (LDWG)

Kana transcription: ノルマ／のるま

Purely phonetic transcription: 野流間　埜留麻
乃瑠真　之琉磨

Purely denotative transcription: 模範 = a pattern, *mohan*;
手本 = a pattern, *tehon*; 見本 = a pattern, *mihon*; 基準量 = a
pattern, *kijunryo* or 模型 = model, *mokei*; 原型 = model, *genkei*.

Phonetic & denotative transcription: 乃留真 = an axiom = "pattern,
model"; 濃留真 = thick truth = "pattern, model."

Phonetic & eulogistic transcription: 能留真 = one who is really
capable; 脳妻磨 = one who often improves his mind; 農留真 =
one who remains a real farmer.

Attention-getting transcription: 能留馬 = a capable horse; 野留魔
= a demon in the field; 乗馬 = a riding horse.

Brainteaser: 否留魔 = No demon permitted here. Note: "No-" (= no)
= 否 in Japanese. Hence it is read "Norma."

Norman
(m) Old English, "Northman" (EGW)

Kana transcription: ノーマン／のーまん

Purely phonetic transcription: 脳万　農満　能慢
濃漫　納鰻　悩蔓

Purely denotative transcription: 北方人 = a Northman,
hoppo-jin; 北国人 = a Northman, *kitaguni-jin*.

Phonetic & denotative transcription: 野宇孟 = a tall man from the
edge of the world = hence "Northman."

Phonetic & eulogistic transcription: 能満 = one who is full of
abilities; 脳万 = one who has thousands of brains; 農真員 = a real
farmer; 農豊満 = a rich farmer.

Attention-getting transcription: 野王鰻 = the king of eels in the
field; 脳鰻 = a wise eel; 悩満 = one who is full of troubles; 悩蟇
運 = a troubled toad's luck.

Oliver
(m) Latin, from "olive" (ECS)

Kana transcription: オリヴァー／おりヴぁー
Purely phonetic transcription: 緒吏場阿　尾利馬雅
御理羽亜　雄璃馬阿　小里魔亜　折場亜
Purely denotative transcription: 阿列布 = olive, *oribu*.
Phonetic & denotative transcription: 阿列布亜 = an
Asian olive = hence "olive."

Phonetic & eulogistic transcription: 雄理罵 = a wise hero who is
shouting; 王利馬 = a clever king on the horse; 夫璃磨 = a
husband who polishes gems; 尾麗羽 = a bird with a beautiful tail;
大吏豊雅 = a great rich and elegant official; 雄理武雅 = a
heroic, wise and elegant samurai.

Attention-getting transcription: 悪狸魔 = a devilishly bad badger;
汚浬場蛙 = a frog in a dirty water zone; 尾狸馬唖 = a badger tail
which is laughed at by a horse; 悪利馬 = a bad, but clever horse;
烏狸罵唖 = a crow condemns and laughs at a badger,

Olivia
(f) Feminine form of Oliver (EGW); see Oliver

Kana transcription: オリヴィア／おりびあ
Purely phonetic transcription: 緒吏美婀　尾利毘雅
御理魅亜　雄璃琵阿
Purely denotative transcription: See Oliver
Phonetic & denotative transcription: 阿列布違亜 = an
Asian olive of different sort = hence "olive"; 阿列布移亜 =
an olive transplanted to Asia = hence "olive."

Phonetic & eulogistic transcription: 雄理魅婀 = a heroic, wise and
charming beauty; 小吏備雅 = a minor official endowed with
elegance; 大璃備雅 = a large and elegant gem; 小麗備婀 = a
small beauty endowed with elegance.

Attention-getting transcription: 悪狸美亜 = a beautiful, but bad
Asian badger; 小狸肥唖 = a small fat laughing badger; 悪利備婀
= a beauty endowed with bad wisdom.

Oscar (m) Old English, "divine"; "spear" (ECS)

Kana transcription: オスカー／おすかー

Purely phonetic transcription: 尾州加雅　尾利馬雅
御理羽亜　雄璃馬阿　小里魔亜　汚離罵雅

Purely denotative transcription: 神槍 = a divine, spear,
kami-yari; 神扠 = a divine, spear, *kami-yasu*; 神聖鎗 = a divine,
spear, *kami-yari*.

Phonetic & denotative transcription: 御槍荷 = in charge of a divine
spear - hence "divine, spear."

Phonetic & eulogistic transcription: 王寿誇 = a king proud of his
longevity; 大主佳雅 = an elegant great lord who is good; 雄司誇
雅 = a heroic official who is proud of elegance; 皇寿家 = a long-
living imperial family.

Attention-getting transcription: 尾雛誇雅 = a fledgling which is
proud of its elegant tail; 牡鹿雅 = an elegant male deer; 雄誇蛙 =
a proud male frog.

Brainteaser: 雄車 = a male car; 汚司車 = a dirty official's car.
Note: "Os-" (osu) = male = 雄 and "-car" = 車 in Japanese. Hence
both are read "Oscar."

Owen (m) Welsh, "wellborn" (LDWG)

Kana transcription: オーウエン／おーうえん

Purely phonetic transcription: 王園　大炎　応宴
欧円　央演　皇縁　鴎援

Purely denotative transcription: See Eugine

Phonetic & denotative transcription: 皇縁 = a relative of the
emperor = hence "wellborn"; 王員 = a royal member = "wellborn."

Phonetic & eulogistic transcription: 王援 = a supporter of the king;
大演 = one who puts on a great performance = hence a great actor;
皇演 = the emperor makes a speech; 追縁 = one who looks for a
spouse; 大宴 = a big banquet.

Attention-getting transcription: 鴨宴 = a feast of wild ducks; 鶯演
= a nightingale's performance; 鷹園 = an eagle's garden.

Patricia

(f) Feminine form of Patrick (RGS); see Patrick

Kana transcription: パトリシア／ぱとりしあ

Purely phonetic transcription: 葉都利指阿
巴渡里詩亜　覇途吏志雅　顔鳥枝唖

Purely denotative transcription: See Patrick

Phonetic & denotative transcription: 伯頭利姉雅 = the elegant elder sister of a leading noble = hence a "patrician."

Phonetic & eulogistic transcription: 顔頭利姉雅 = an elegant elder sister who is very clever; 覇土離使婀 = a beauty who leaves the conquered land as a messenger; 伯討麗示婀 = an elegant beauty who plans to attack the duke.

Attention-getting transcription: 歯取獅阿 = an African lion whose teeth have been pulled out; 破頭霊脂亜 = a fat Asian ghost whose head has been broken; 羽取獅阿 = an African lion which catches birds; 波到狸子唖 = a baby badger which laughs at the arriving waves; 把兎利獅亜 = a clever Asian lion which catches a rabbit.

Patrick

(m) Latin, "patrician" (RGS)

Kana transcription: パトリック／ぱとりっく

Purely phonetic transcription: 葉都利駆　巴渡里句
破戸離供　羽頭理究　波吐浬貢　顔鳥倶

Purely denotative transcription: 貴族 = noble class, *kizoku*; 高貴 = noble, *koki*; 貴戚 = noble, *kiseki*; 貴尊 = noble, *kison*; 貴人 = a noble person, *kijin*.

Phonetic & denotative transcription: 伯頭利公 = a wise count = hence a "patrician."

Phonetic & eulogistic transcription: 覇討離駆 = one who conquers and drives the enemies away; 顔頭理公 = a duke who is very wise; 破倒離苦 = one who defeats troubles.

Attention-getting transcription: 破頭霊苦 = a broken-headed ghost which suffers pain; 羽取狗 = a dog which catches birds; 把兎狸駆 = a badger which runs to catch a rabbit.

Patsy

(f) Pet form of Patricia (LDWG); see Patrick

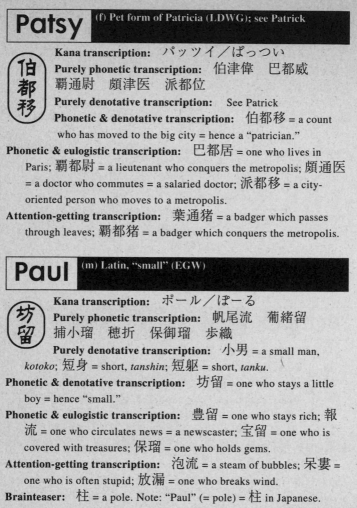

Kana transcription: パッツイ／ぱっつい

Purely phonetic transcription: 伯津偉　巴都威　覇通尉　顚津医　派都位

Purely denotative transcription: See Patrick

Phonetic & denotative transcription: 伯都移 = a count who has moved to the big city = hence a "patrician."

Phonetic & eulogistic transcription: 巴都居 = one who lives in Paris; 覇都尉 = a lieutenant who conquers the metropolis; 顚通医 = a doctor who commutes = a salaried doctor; 派都移 = a city-oriented person who moves to a metropolis.

Attention-getting transcription: 葉通猪 = a badger which passes through leaves; 覇都猪 = a badger which conquers the metropolis.

Paul

(m) Latin, "small" (EGW)

Kana transcription: ポール／ぽーる

Purely phonetic transcription: 帆尾流　葡緒留　捕小瑠　穂折　保御瑠　歩織

Purely denotative transcription: 小男 = a small man, *kotoko*; 短身 = short, *tanshin*; 短躯 = short, *tanku*.

Phonetic & denotative transcription: 坊留 = one who stays a little boy = hence "small."

Phonetic & eulogistic transcription: 豊留 = one who stays rich; 報流 = one who circulates news = a newscaster; 宝留 = one who is covered with treasures; 保瑠 = one who holds gems.

Attention-getting transcription: 泡流 = a steam of bubbles; 呆妻 = one who is often stupid; 放漏 = one who breaks wind.

Brainteaser: 柱 = a pole. Note: "Paul" (= pole) = 柱 in Japanese. Hence it is read "Paul."

Paula

(f) German, feminine form of Paul (EGW); see Paul

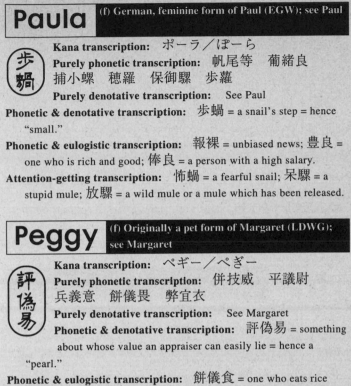

Kana transcription: ポーラ／ぽーら

Purely phonetic transcription: 帆尾等　葡緒良　捕小螺　穂羅　保御騾　歩蘿

Purely denotative transcription: See Paul

Phonetic & denotative transcription: 歩蝸 = a snail's step = hence "small."

Phonetic & eulogistic transcription: 報裸 = unbiased news; 豊良 = one who is rich and good; 俸良 = a person with a high salary.

Attention-getting transcription: 怖蝸 = a fearful snail; 呆騾 = a stupid mule; 放騾 = a wild mule or a mule which has been released.

Peggy

(f) Originally a pet form of Margaret (LDWG); see Margaret

Kana transcription: ペギー／ぺぎー

Purely phonetic transcription: 併技威　平議尉　兵義意　餅儀畏　弊宜衣

Purely denotative transcription: See Margaret

Phonetic & denotative transcription: 評偽易 = something about whose value an appraiser can easily lie = hence a "pearl."

Phonetic & eulogistic transcription: 餅儀食 = one who eats rice cakes at a ceremony; 陛儀衣 = an empress in ceremonial clothes; 平義医 = a regular voluntary doctor.

Attention-getting transcription: 餅蟻食 = an ant which eats a rice cake; 並着衣 = one who wears normal clothes; 幣偽移 = one who circulates false money.

Penelope
(f) Greek, "pene a bobbin," in reference to the thread on a bobbin (LDWG)

糸巻

Kana transcription: ペネーロペ／ぺねーろぺ

Purely phonetic transcription: 併値路兵　平根露塀
兵襴呂弊　餅音櫓並

Purely denotative transcription: 糸巻 = a bobbin, *itomaki*;
機織女 = a weaver, *hataori-onna*; 織婦 = a weaver, *shoku-fu*; 機
婦 = a weaver, *kifu*; 織姫 = a weaver, *orihime*.

Phonetic & denotative transcription: 蔽寧労柄 = a hidden handle
which works painstakingly = hence a "bobbin" of a weaving machine.

Phonetic & eulogistic transcription: 平寧朗侶嬰 = a very polite,
cheerful and lovable wife; 陛子侶並 = a prince's spouse = hence a
princess; 併寧良妃 = a princess who is good and polite as well.

Attention-getting transcription: 並寝虜悲 = sad prisoners who
sleep in a line.

Peter
(m) Greek, "stone, rock" (RGS)

岩石

Kana transcription: ピーター／ぴーたー

Purely phonetic transcription: 兵位田亜　併威多雅
平偉太阿　蔽畏汰亜

Purely denotative transcription: 石 = a stone, *ishi*; 石塊 =
a stone, *ishikoro*; 地骨 = a stone, *chikotsu* or 岩 = a rock, *iwa*; 岩
石 = a stone and a rock, *genseki*; 巌磐 = a rock, *ganban*.

Phonetic & denotative transcription: 塀井多 = many are used to
build a well wall = hence "stones"; 蔽囲田闕 = things which
surround the rice field = hence "stones."

Phonetic & eulogistic transcription: 平威他 = one who conquers
others by threats; 陛多雅 = Your Majesty, full of elegance; 評易
他 = one who evaluates others easily = a critic.

Attention-getting transcription: 批威他唖 = one who arrogantly
criticizes and laughs at others; 兵移惰雅 = a soldier who becomes
lazy and soft.

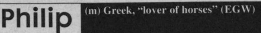

Philip

(m) Greek, "lover of horses" (EGW)

Kana transcription: フィリップ／ふぃりっぷ

Purely phonetic transcription: 符位理符　父異離父　不意里婦　豊畏麗符　富偉吏夫　賦威利布

Purely denotative transcription: 馬好 = a lover of horses, *uma-zuki*; 馬愛好者 = a lover of horses, *uma-aikosha*; 馬愛好家 = a lover of horses, *uma-aikoka*.

Phonetic & denotative transcription: 扶囲鈴撫 = to keep in a corral, pat, and affix bells to (a horse) = hence "lovers of horses."

Phonetic & eulogistic transcription: 富偉利夫 = a rich, great and clever husband; 婦慰理夫 = a wise husband who consoles his wife; 豊威吏補 = a rich and dignified official.

Attention-getting transcription: 怖猪利富 = a fearful, but clever rich wild boar; 撫胃狸父 = a badger father which rubs its stomach; 夫猪離婦 = a badger husband which divorces its wife.

Phyllis

(f) Greek, "leafy" (EGW)

葉子

Kana transcription: フィリス／ふぃりす

Purely phonetic transcription: 符位理州　父異離巣　不意里諏　豊畏麗須　富偉吏寿　賦威利簾

Purely denotative transcription: 葉 = a leaf, *ha*; 葉身 = a leaf, *yoshin*; 葉子 = a leaf, *yoshi*; 木葉 = a leaf of the tree, *moku-yo*; 樹葉 = a leaf of the tree, *ju-yo*.

Phonetic & denotative transcription: 豊葦麗洲 = abundant beautiful reeds in the sand bank = hence "leafy."

Phonetic & eulogistic transcription: 豊威理寿 = one who is rich, dignified, wise and long-living; 婦偉麗素 = a great, graceful and honest woman; 婦医利素 = a clever and honest woman doctor; 婦位俐主 = a clever lady hostess.

Attention-getting transcription: 豊猪里雛 = a fledgling in a rich wild boar land; 撫猪狸子 = one who pets a badger cub.

Polly

(f) Originally a pet form of Mary (LDWG); see Mary

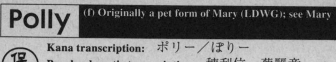

Kana transcription: ポリー／ぽりー

Purely phonetic transcription: 穂利位　葡麗意　帆浬移　布璃畏　保吏威　補履

Purely denotative transcription: See Mary

Phonetic & denotative transcription: 歩離移 = one who has to walk away, leaving (his family) = hence "bitterness"

Phonetic & eulogistic transcription: 保麗 = one who maintains elegance; 輔利医 = a clever assistant doctor; 豊理偉 = one who is rich, wise and great; 保礼 = one who maintains courtesy.

Attention-getting transcription: 怖狸異 = a fearful strange badger; 捕鯉井 = one who catches carp in the well; 保吏威 = an official who keeps his dignity.

Quincy

(m) Old French, Latin, name of a village; "fifth" (RGS)

Kana transcription: クインシー／くいんしー

Purely phonetic transcription: 宮印士威　久姻施偉　俱院詩位　究蔭氏畏　玖韻使移　句引誌慰　区員師衣 or 宮印士　久姻施　俱院詩　究蔭氏

Purely denotative transcription: 第五 = fifth, *daigo*; 五番 = fifth, *goban*; 五番目 = fifth, *gobanme*; 五男 = the fifth son, *gonan*.

Phonetic & denotative transcription: 丘陰芝囲 = an lawn enclosure behind the hill = hence an "estate"; 九引四位 = the position which results from deducting four from nine = hence "fifth."

Phonetic & eulogistic transcription: 公胤師偉 = a great teacher who is a royal descendant; 功引侍威 = a dignified samurai who draws merit; 救員歯医 = a dentist who saves people.

Attention-getting transcription: 鳩飲脂異 = a pigeon which drinks strange fat; 駒姻脂猪 = a horse which marries a fat wild boar; 狗引髭猪 = a dog which pulls a wild boar's beard; 駈隠獅葦 = a lion which runs into the reeds to hide.

Ralph
(m) Old English, compound of "counsel" and "wolf" (EGW)

Kana transcription: ラルフ／らるふ

Purely phonetic transcription: 羅瑠譜　等流賦　螺留豊　良留膚　羅琉劉富

Purely denotative transcription: 助言狼 = counsel and wolf, *jogen-ro*; 忠告狼 = counsel and wolf, *chukoku-ro*; 勧告狼 = counsel and wolf, *kankoku-okami*.

Phonetic & denotative transcription: 裸狼怖 = a fearful naked wolf = hence a "wolf"; 等流歩 = those which are nomadic = hence "wolves"; 裸留輔 = one who helps those poorly clothed, wretched people = hence "counsel."

Phonetic & eulogistic transcription: 良瑠豊 = one who owns plenty of good gems; 良留夫 = a good husband.

Attention-getting transcription: 驟婁怖 = a mule which is often fearful; 乱流布 = one who casts false rumors.

Raymond
(M) Germanic, compound of "counsel," and "protection" (RGS)

Kana transcription: レイモンド／れいもんど

Purely phonetic transcription: 霊門土　令紋度　礼文努　励問怒　麗問土　鈴悶度　玲聞度

Purely denotative transcription: 助言保護 = counsel and protection, *jogen-hogo*; 忠告守護 = counsel and protection, *chukoku-shugo*; 勧告護衛 = counsel and protection, *kankoku-goei*; 弁護士警護 = counsel and protection, *bengoshi-keigo*.

Phonetic & denotative transcription: 励聞度 = one who listens to and encourages (people) = hence "counsel"; 励武運導 = one who seeks to bring good luck militarily = hence "protection."

Phonetic & eulogistic transcription: 礼文努 = one who learns courtesy and culture; 零悶怒 = one who is never troubled and never angry; 怜問努 = one who tries hard to ask wise questions.

Attention-getting transcription: 霊悶怒 = an angry ghost who is troubled; 領聞動 = a president who listens and then takes action.

Rebecca
(f) Hebrew, "a cord with a noose"; "a snare" (HS)

係蹄

Kana transcription: レベッカ／れべっか

Purely phonetic transcription: 麗部加　玲琶佳
礼辺香　嶺部賀　伶琶華

Purely denotative transcription: 罠 = a snare, *wana*; 係蹄
= a snare, *keitei*; 筌蹄 = a snare, *sentei*.

Phonetic & denotative transcription: 嶺辺掛 = something that is set
near the ridge = hence a "snare."

Phonetic & eulogistic transcription: 麗辺佳 = a beauty in the
neighborhood; 礼部嫁 = a polite bride in the village; 伶魅嫁 = a
wise and charming bride.

Attention-getting transcription: 霊美歌 = a ghost's beautiful song;
零米嫁 = a riceless (= foodless) bride; 鈴辺嘩 = a bell ringing
noisily in the neighborhood; 零魅嫁 = a charmless bride; 麗屁嫁
= an elegant bride who breaks wind.

Reggie
(m) Germanic, "might, power" (ECS)

励侍

Kana transcription: レジー／れじー

Purely phonetic transcription: 礼治威　伶自畏
嶺慈猪　玲侍偉　霊持維　励滋尉　伶辞易

Purely denotative transcription: 力 = might, power,
chikara; 勢力 = might, power, *seiryoku*; 能力 = might, power,
noryoku; 力量 = might, power, *seiryoku*.

Phonetic & denotative transcription: 励侍偉 = a distinguished
samurai making great efforts = hence "might, power"; 領治威 = a
president who rules with dignity = hence "might, power."

Phonetic & eulogistic transcription: 礼慈医 = a courteous and
benevolent doctor; 怜示威 = one who shows wisdom and dignity;
麗尼偉 = a great nun who is graceful; 励持医 = an industrious
doctor.

Attention-getting transcription: 零児猪 = a childless wild boar; 零
値医 = a worthless doctor; 霊慈威 = a great ghost who is
benevolent.

142

Richard
(m) Germanic, compound of "rule" and "hard" (RGS)

Kana transcription: リチャード／りちゃーど

Purely phonetic transcription: 理知雅努　麗智亜度　履値阿土　利茶亜努　理茶阿怒　履茶雅度

Purely denotative transcription: 統治厳格 = rule and hard, *tochi-genkaku*; 支配苛酷 = rule and hard, *shihai-kakoku*.

Phonetic & denotative transcription: 吏治雅土 = an official who rules an elegant land = hence "rule"; 里治雅努 = one who strives to rule the village elegantly.

Phonetic & eulogistic transcription: 理智雅努 = one who tries to be wise and elegant; 吏治亜土 = an official who rules an Asian land.

Attention-getting transcription: 利蜘唖度 = a clever spider which often laughs; 鯉痴唖努 = a stupid carp which tries to laugh.

Robert
(m) Old English, French, compound of "fame" and "bright" (EGW)

Kana transcription: ロバート／ろばーと

Purely phonetic transcription: 露場亜頭　呂芭阿渡　路馬雅都　櫓魔跡　慮鳩

Purely denotative transcription: 名声燦然 = fame and bright, *meisei-sanzen*; 高名耀照 = fame and bright, *komei-yosho*; 盛名輝耀 = fame and bright, *seimei-kiyo*.

Phonetic & denotative transcription: 良豊雅灯 = a good, rich and elegant light = hence "bright"; 慮磨雅頭 = to place an emphasis on keeping one's mind polished = hence "bright"; 炉場雅灯 = a furnace which can also be a bright light = "bright."

Phonetic & eulogistic transcription: 良磨雅宕 = one who polishes precious stones elegantly; 侶羽雅杜 = an elegant feathered companion in the woods; 朗豊雅頭 = a boss who is cheerful, rich and elegant.

Attention-getting transcription: 驢馬蛙妬 = a donkey which is jealous of a frog; 鷺罵鴉度 = a heron which frequently condemns a crow; 魯馬唖兎 = a foolish horse which often laughs at a rabbit.

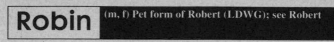

Robin

(m, f) Pet form of Robert (LDWG); see Robert

Kana transcription: ロビン／ろびん

Purely phonetic transcription: 露魅引　旅琶韻
櫨美蔭　櫓備員　慮敏　炉便

Purely denotative transcription: See Robert

Phonetic & denotative transcription: 炉火引 = to ignite a furnace =
hence "bright"; 露日引 = a dew drop reflecting the sun = hence
"bright."

Phonetic & eulogistic transcription: 朗魅員 = a cheerful and
charming person; 慮美韻 = one who sounds considerate and
beautiful; 露美隠 = a dew drop in which beauty is hidden; 郎敏 =
a swift man.

Attention-getting transcription: 驢肥隠 = a fat donkey which is
hiding; 鷺貧 = a poor heron; 魯肥員 = a foolish fat person; 狼尾
隠 = a wolf which hides its tail.

Roger

**(m) Germanic, compound of "fame" and "spear"
(RGS)**

Kana transcription: ロジャー／ろじゃー

Purely phonetic transcription: 炉治雅　路侍阿
露慈亜　櫓示雅　蕗児亜　虜者　魯邪　漏蒔

Purely denotative transcription: 名声槍 = fame and spear,
meisei-so; 高名扠 = fame and spear, *komei-sa*; 令聞槍 = fame and
spear, *meibun-so*; 名望扠 = fame and spear, *meibo-yasu*; 有名槍 =
a famous spear, *yumei-yari*; 有名扠 = a famous spear, *yumei-yasu*.

Phonetic & denotative transcription: 櫓射雅 = what is elegantly
shot from the castle turret = hence a "spear."

Phonetic & eulogistic transcription: 慮侍雅 = a considerate and
elegant samurai; 朗児雅 = a cheerful and elegant child; 良治亜 =
one who rules Asia well; 郎慈雅 = a benevolent and elegant man.

Attention-getting transcription: 魯侍唖 = a stupid samurai who is
laughing; 露慈蛙 = a frog which shows benevolence; 竜治鴉 = a
dragon which rules crows; 朗蛇 = a cheerful snake.

Ronald

(m) Scottish form of Reginald (EGW); see Reggie

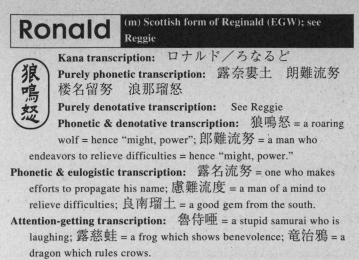

Kana transcription: ロナルド／ろなるど

Purely phonetic transcription: 露奈妻土　朗難流努
楼名留努　浪那瑠怒

Purely denotative transcription: See Reggie

Phonetic & denotative transcription: 狼鳴怒 = a roaring
wolf = hence "might, power"; 郎難流努 = a man who
endeavors to relieve difficulties = hence "might, power."

Phonetic & eulogistic transcription: 露名流努 = one who makes
efforts to propagate his name; 慮難流度 = a man of a mind to
relieve difficulties; 良南瑠土 = a good gem from the south.

Attention-getting transcription: 魯侍唖 = a stupid samurai who is
laughing; 露慈蛙 = a frog which shows benevolence; 竜治鴉 = a
dragon which rules crows.

Ronnie

(m) Pet form of Ronald (LDWG); see Ronald

Purely phonetic transcription: 露丹畏　朗仁意
慮児移　浪忍尉　侶荷衣

Purely denotative transcription: See Ronald/Reggie

Phonetic & denotative transcription: 狼児威 = a wolf
which threatens a child = hence "might, power"; 慮侍偉 = a
great samurai who is considerate = hence "might, power."

Phonetic & eulogistic transcription: 慮仁医 = a considerate and
benevolent doctor; 旅児偉 = a great child who travels; 侶丹衣 = a
priest in red clothes.

Attention-getting transcription: 侶尼威 = a priest who threatens a
nun; 魯児 = a stupid child.

Rose

(f) Although long identified with the flower, it actually is a derivative of "horse" (EGW)

楼図

Kana transcription: ローズ／ろーず

Purely phonetic transcription: 露緒逗　朗豆　楼図　浪逗　篭途　滝頭　蝋厨

Purely denotative transcription: 薔薇 = rose, *shika*; 刺花 = rose, *shika* or 馬 = a horse, *uma*; 天駒 = a horse, *tenku*; 天蹄 = a horse, *tentei*; 雷足 = a horse, *raisoku*; 駒 = a horse, *koma*.

Phonetic & denotative transcription: 旅王途 = a king on a journey = on a "horse"; 露生逗 = where dew drops are born = on a "rose."

Phonetic & eulogistic transcription: 慮旺徒 = a very considerate person; 朗頭 = a cheerful boss; 朗瞳 = one who has cheerful eyes.

Attention-getting transcription: 浪鴨逗 = a wild duck staying in the waves; 朗鴬杜 = a cheerful nightingale in the forest; 露優頭 = a beautiful dew drop (falling) on a head.

Rosemary

(f) An alteration of *rosemarine*, "dew of the sea" (LDWG)

海露

Kana transcription: ローズマリー／ろーずまりー

Purely phonetic transcription: 朗豆磨利　楼図麻麗　浪逗摩璃　篭途馬里　滝頭間梨　蝋厨魔離

Purely denotative transcription: 海露 = dew of the sea, *kairo*; 海洋露玉 = dew of the sea, *kaiyo-rogyoku*; 大洋露珠 = dew of the sea, *taiyo-roshu*; 冥海玉露 = dew of the sea, *meikai-gyokuro*; 碧海露滴 = dew of the sea, *hekikai-roteki*.

Phonetic & denotative transcription: 露生逗真雅蛎 = dew drops born to stay where truly beautiful oysters live = "dew of the sea."

Phonetic & eulogistic transcription: 慮旺徒真利 = a very considerate person who is really clever; 朗頭真麗 = a cheerful boss who is elegant; 朗瞳磨璃 = one who has cheerful eyes which look like polished gems.

Attention-getting transcription: 浪鴨逗間浬 = wild ducks, scattered miles apart, floating stationary on the waves; 朗鴬杜真理 = a cheerful and very wise nightingale in the forest.

Roy

(m) Celtic, Old French, "red"; "king" (ECS)

露威

Kana transcription: ロイ／ろい

Purely phonetic transcription: 露意　路畏　慮慰　呂偉　櫓威　魯位　蕗衣

Purely denotative transcription: 赤王 = red king, *seki-o*; 紅赤帝王 = red king, *koseki-teio*; 赤毛王 = a red-haired king, *akage-o*; 赤顔王様 = a red-faced king, *akagao-osama*.

Phonetic & denotative transcription: 露威 = one who exposes dignity = hence a "king"; 露位 = one who exposes his rank = hence a "king"; 露偉 = one who shows greatness = hence a "king."

Phonetic & eulogistic transcription: 侶偉 = a great spouse; 朗威 = one who is cheerful and dignified; 良医 = a good doctor.

Attention-getting transcription: 鷺偉 = a great heron; 虜威 = a dignified prisoner; 竜畏 = a respected dragon.

Rudolph

(m) Germanic, "famous wolf" (GRS)

名声狼

Kana transcription: ルドルフ／るどるふ

Purely phonetic transcription: 留度留富　流土流豊　琉努琉賦　瑠怒瑠譜

Purely denotative transcription: 名声狼 = famous wolf, *meisei-ro*; 高名狼 = famous wolf, *komei-ro*; 令聞狼 = famous wolf, *meibun-ro* or 有名狼 = a famous wolf, *yumei-okami*; 名望狼 = famous wolf, *meibo-okami*.

Phonetic & denotative transcription: 狼怒留怖 = a wolf which lingers and roars fearfully = hence a "wolf"; 狼怒流布 = a roaring wolf whose reputation is spreading = hence "famous wolf."

Phonetic & eulogistic transcription: 瑠土留豊 = one who is rich in the land of gems; 瑠堂留夫 = a husband who stays in a gem shop; 留努留豊 = one who tries hard to remain rich.

Attention-getting transcription: 留怒流布 = one who is angry about a rumor; 流動婁夫 = a husband who is often unstable; 流動婁富 = a fortune which changes often.

Russell

(m) French, "a red-haired or red-faced man" (LDWG)

Kana transcription: ラッセル／らっせる

Purely phonetic transcription: 羅寿　等巣　螺須　良諏 or 羅瀬瑠　等施留　螺世琉　良勢流

Purely denotative transcription: 可愛赤 = little red, *kawai-aka*; 赤頭 = a red head, *aka-atama*; 赤毛 = red hair, *aka-atama*; 赤髪 = a red head, *aka-ge*; 赤頭髪 = a red head, *aka-tohatsu*; 丹朱毛 = a red head, *tanshu-mo*.

Phonetic & denotative transcription: 郎朱留 = a man who has always been of ruddy complexion = hence a "red-haired man."

Phonetic & eulogistic transcription: 良正留 = one who remains good and true; 良婿留 = a good bridegroom; 等誠留 = sincere ones.

Attention-getting transcription: 螺瀬留 = a shell on the shore; 驟誠留 = a sincere mule; 蝸聖留 = a sacred snail.

Brainteaser: 螺売 = a shell seller. Note: "-ssell" (= to sell) = 売 in Japanese. Hence it is read "Russell."

Sally

(f) Originally a pet form of Sarah (LDWG); see Sarah

Kana transcription: サリー／さりー

Purely phonetic transcription: 差吏位　査璃移　瑳麗威　紗裏維　唆理偉

Purely denotative transcription: See Sarah

Phonetic & denotative transcription: 沙麗衣 = one who wears an elegant silk dress = hence "my princess"; 差麗偉 = one who has a great difference in elegance = hence a "my princess."

Phonetic & eulogistic transcription: 瑳麗威 = one who practices elegance and dignity; 瑳麗慰 = one who consoles by smiling elegantly; 査璃移 = one who travels to look for gems; 作婀麗 = a beauty whose manners are elegant.

Attention-getting transcription: 蹉婀利 = a clever beauty who stumbles; 挫利猪 = a clever wild boar which suffers a failure; 唆婀吏 = a beauty who seduces an official.

Samantha
(f) Feminine form of Samuel (LDWG); see Samuel

Kana transcription: サマンサ／さまんさ

Purely phonetic transcription: 差満再　査万紗　紗蔓査　唆漫瑳　瑳慢茶

Purely denotative transcription: See Samuel

Phonetic & denotative transcription: 作万差 = to make thousands of differences = "His name is God"; 査万詐 = to inspect thousands of frauds = "His name is God."

Phonetic & eulogistic transcription: 査蹒挫 = one who checks for cheating and stops it; 作満茶 = a tea planter; 瑳満茶 = one who pours tea with a smile; 紗満作 = one who makes a lot of clothes.

Attention-getting transcription: 砂鰻嗟 = an eel which sighs in the sand; 作万唆 = one who makes ten thousand temptations.

Samuel
(m) Hebrew, "His name is God"; "name of God"; "God hath heard" (ECS)

Kana transcription: サミュエル／さみゅえる

Purely phonetic transcription: 差実油絵流　査身湯江琉　紗未愉柄留　唆魅恵瑠　沙美諭慧漏

Purely denotative transcription: 神名 = the name of God, *jinmei*; 神名号 = the name of God, *jin-meigo* 神乃御名 = the name of God, *kami-no-mina*; or 神上聞 = God hath heard, *kami-jomon*; 神叡聞 = God hath heard, *kami-eibun*; 神天聴 = God hath heard, *kami-tencho*.

Phonetic & denotative transcription: 尊名恵留 = the respected name which stays benevolent = hence "His name is God."

Phonetic & eulogistic transcription: 査務慧留 = a wise inspector; 作武得 = one who has obtained samurai manners; 作夢得 = one who makes his dreams come true; 瑳武栄留 = a smiling prosperous samurai.

Attention-getting transcription: 挫夢永留 = one who fails in his eternal dream; 寒泳留 = one who swims in the cold weather; 作夢栄留 = one who achieves prosperity in a dream.

Sandra

(f) Italian diminutive of Alexandra (EGW); see Alexander

参導良

Kana transcription: サンドラ／さんどら

Purely phonetic transcription: 賛努等　参童良 散動蝸　讃同喇　山土蘿

Purely denotative transcription: See Alexander

Phonetic & denotative transcription: 参導良 = one who comes to guide people well = hence a "defending man"; 惨導良 = one who guides misery to good = hence a "defending man."

Phonetic & eulogistic transcription: 賛同裸 = one who agrees to be naked; 参堂良 = one who pays many visits to a shrine; 燦童良 = a bright good child; 産農良 = a farmer who is producing well.

Attention-getting transcription: 惨怒騾 = a wretched angry mule; 餐農等 = farmers having dinner.

Sarah

(f) Hebrew, "my princess" (HS)

更雅

Kana transcription: サラー／さらー

Purely phonetic transcription: 差羅雅　査等阿 瑳螺亜　紗良雅　唆羅阿

Purely denotative transcription: 妃殿下 = my princess, *hidenka*; 王女 = a princess, *ojo*; 皇女 = a princess, *kojo*; 王妃 = a princess, *ohi*; 親王妃 = a princess, *shinnohi*.

Phonetic & denotative transcription: 紗羅雅 = one who wears an elegant silk dress = hence "my princess."

Phonetic & eulogistic transcription: 紗良 = good cloth; 査良雅 = a good elegant inspector; 瑳良 = a good polisher; 更雅 = one who is even more elegant.

Attention-getting transcription: 蹉騾阿 = a stumbling African mule; 嗟喇雅 = a sighing elegant trumpet; 皿唖 = a laughing dish; 査騾雅 = an elegant mule inspector.

Brainteaser: 爵裸 = a naked countess. Note: "Sa-" (= Sir) = 爵 in Japanese. Hence it is read "Sarah."

150

Scot

(m) Celtic, one from Scotland or Ireland (ECS)

Kana transcription: スコット／すこっと

Purely phonetic transcription: 諏誇都　州湖渡　須子戸　寿呼頭　数虎途　素鼓塗　簾庫戸　酢古杜

Purely denotative transcription: 蘇格蘭人 = a Scot, *sukottorando-jin* or 愛蘭人 = an Irishman, *airurando-jin*.

Phonetic & denotative transcription: 蘇格渡 = one who came over from Scotland = hence "one from Scotland."

Phonetic & eulogistic transcription: 寿誇頭 = a boss who boasts of longevity; 素子都 = an honest urban child; 崇皇刀 = a solemn royal sword; 主護都 = a lord who defends the capital; 守皇頭 = a boss who defends the emperor.

Attention-getting transcription: 寿狐杜 = a long-living fox in the forest; 素誇兎 = a proud simple rabbit; 守虎頭 = a boss with a tiger.

Brainteaser: 素家 = a simple house; 雛家 = the house of fledglings. Note: "-cot" = 家 in Japanese. Hence both are read "Scot."

Sean

(m) Irish form of John through Norman-French Jean (EGW); see John

Kana transcription: ショーン／しょーん

Purely phonetic transcription: 曙穏　初恩　書苑　渚園　諸音　処温　庶怨

Purely denotative transcription: See John

Phonetic & denotative transcription: 初御恩 = the first gracious favor = hence "gracious gift of God."

Phonetic & eulogistic transcription: 曙穏 = a mild sunrise; 照恩 = a brilliant favor; 将飲 = a general who drinks (a lot); 勝運 = luck in victory.

Attention-getting transcription: 鼠隠 = a hiding rat; 薯温 = a warm potato.

Sharon
(f) Hebrew, "plain" or "level country" (ECS)

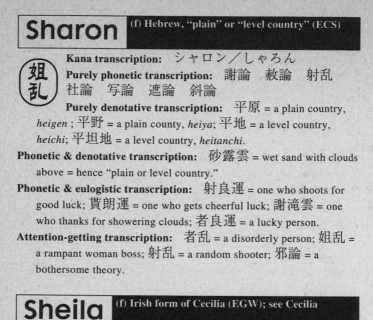

姐乱

Kana transcription: シャロン／しゃろん

Purely phonetic transcription: 謝論　赦論　射乱
社論　写論　遮論　斜論

Purely denotative transcription: 平原 = a plain country, *heigen*; 平野 = a plain county, *heiya*; 平地 = a level country, *heichi*; 平坦地 = a level country, *heitanchi*.

Phonetic & denotative transcription: 砂露雲 = wet sand with clouds above = hence "plain or level country."

Phonetic & eulogistic transcription: 射良運 = one who shoots for good luck; 賞朗運 = one who gets cheerful luck; 謝滝雲 = one who thanks for showering clouds; 者良運 = a lucky person.

Attention-getting transcription: 者乱 = a disorderly person; 姐乱 = a rampant woman boss; 射乱 = a random shooter; 邪論 = a bothersome theory.

Sheila
(f) Irish form of Cecilia (EGW); see Cecilia

視壊等

Kana transcription: シェーラ／しぇーら

Purely phonetic transcription: 詩絵蝸　司慧等
姿映良　紫廻蘿　指衛喇

Purely denotative transcription: See Cecilia

Phonetic & denotative transcription: 視壊等 = those whose vision has been destroyed = hence "blind."

Phonetic & eulogistic transcription: 獅英裸 = a bright naked lioness; 姉恵良 = a good and benevolent elder sister; 子泳裸 = naked children who are swimming; 子慧良 = a clever and good child; 詩詠良 = one who sings good poems = hence a good poet.

Attention-getting transcription: 脂慧騾 = a fat wise mule; 刺衛蘿 = ivy which defends itself with thorns.

Sherry

(f) French, "dear one" (LDWG)

Kana transcription: シェリー／しぇりー

Purely phonetic transcription: 師江里位　誌絵利異　詩慧理意　資柄梨畏　試衛璃偉　姿恵麗

Purely denotative transcription: 親愛人 = dear one, *shin-aijin*; 親好者 = dear one, *shinko-sha*; 和親者 = dear one, *shinwa-sha*; 親情人 = dear one, *shinjo-nin*; 愛人 = a lover, *aijin*; 恋人 = a sweetheart, *koibito*; 情人 = a sweetheart, *jojin*.

Phonetic & denotative transcription: 思恵麗 = one who thinks of benevolence and elegance = hence "dear one."

Phonetic & eulogistic transcription: 姉慧麗 = a wise and elegant elder sister; 示恵利 = one who shows benevolence; 施恵吏 = an official who provides benevolence; 紫衣麗威 = one who is elegant and dignified in purple clothes.

Attention-getting transcription: 雌泳霊 = a swimming female ghost; 師詠嶺 = a teacher who makes a poem over the ridge.

Shirley

(f) Common English place name, "bright clearing."

Kana transcription: シャーリー／しゃーりー

Purely phonetic transcription: 謝阿理意　赦雅利威　写亜璃偉　叉履慰　社裏畏

Purely denotative transcription: 明燦空地 = a bright clearing, *meisan-akichi*; 耀明開拓地 = a bright clearing, *yomei-kaitakuchi*.

Phonetic & denotative transcription: 照雅里囲 = a shining elegant enclosed land = hence a "bright clearing."

Phonetic & eulogistic transcription: 者雅利威 = an elegant, clever and dignified person; 姿夜婀麗 = a beauty who has a graceful style at night; 謝婀礼 = a very courteous beauty.

Attention-getting transcription: 姐雅零 = a woman boss with no elegance at all; 這蛙麗 = a elegant crawling frog.

Sidney
(m, f) Celtic, a telescoping of St. Denis (ECS); "the Sacred" (KED)

神聖

Kana transcription: シドニー／しどにー

Purely phonetic transcription: 詩度荷偉　侍努児威　思怒尼位　司導仁医

Purely denotative transcription: 神聖 = sacred, *shinsei*; 清浄 = sacred, pure, *seijo*.

Phonetic & denotative transcription: 神動仁畏 = solemn divine benevolence = hence "sacred"; 神導児畏 = a solemn child guided by God = hence "the Sacred."

Phonetic & eulogistic transcription: 子導仁偉 = a great child leading to benevolence; 神導仁医 = a benevolent doctor guided by God; 侍能仁畏 = an able, benevolent and solemn samurai.

Attention-getting transcription: 獅怒丹威 = a angry red rampant lion; 脂怒尼威 = a fat, angry and arrogant nun; 侍怒荷易 = an angry samurai with a light burden.

Simon
(m) Hebrew, "God has heard"; "hearkening"; "snub-nosed" (ECS)

神聞

Kana transcription: サイモン／さいもん

Purely phonetic transcription: 際門　才問　再紋　最文　祭悶　歳紋　債聞

Purely denotative transcription: 神上聞 = God hath heard, *kami-jomon*; 神叡聞 = God hath heard, *kami-eibun* or 傾聴 = hearkening, *keicho*; 耳聞 = hearkening, *jibun* or 獅子鼻 = a snub-nosed, *shishi-bana*; 団子鼻 = a snub-nosed, *dango-pana*; 趺坐鼻 = a snub-nosed, *agura-bana*.

Phonetic & denotative transcription: 裁聞 = to hear and judge = hence "God has heard"; 採聞 = to hear and take into (account) = hence "hearkening."

Phonetic & eulogistic transcription: 罪問 = to question sins; 才文 = a literary genius; 砕悶 = one who solves problems.

Attention-getting transcription: 催悶 = a troublemaker; 妻問 = one who questions his wife; 犀悶 = a troubled rhinoceros.

154

Sonia
(f) Russian diminutive of Sophia (EGW); see Sophia

Kana transcription: ソニア／そにあ
Purely phonetic transcription: 蘇荷雅　素仁婀
聡児唖　爽耳雅　想尼亜
Purely denotative transcription: See Sophia
Phonetic & denotative transcription: 蘇仁慧雅 = to revive benevolence, wisdom and elegance = hence "wisdom"; 聡尼婀 = a wise and beautiful nun = hence "wisdom."

Phonetic & eulogistic transcription: 操仁婀 = a beauty who handles benevolence; 想尼雅 = an elegant nun who is thinking; 聡児雅 = a wise and elegant child; 奏荷婀 = a beauty who is in charge of playing music.

Attention-getting transcription: 鼠乳婀 = a beauty who milks a rat; 薮牛阿 = an African cow in the bush; 騒尼雅 = a elegant nun who is noisy; 鼠丹亜 = an Asian red rat.

Sophia
(f) Greek, "wisdom" (GRS)

Kana transcription: ソフィア／そふぃあ
Purely phonetic transcription: 蘇扶威雅　素豊偉婀
聡婦位雅　爽風慰阿
Purely denotative transcription: 利口 = wisdom, *riko*; 賢明 = wisdom, *kenmei*; 明敏 = wisdom, *meibin*; 利発 = wisdom, *rihatsu*; 聡明 = wisdom, *somei*; 怜悧 = wisdom, *reiri*.

Phonetic & denotative transcription: 蘇豊慧雅 = to revive rich elegant wisdom = hence "wisdom"; 聡富偉婀 = a great beauty who is wise and rich = hence "wisdom."

Phonetic & eulogistic transcription: 操富移婀 = a beauty who handles fortunes; 聡婦偉雅 = a great woman who is wise and elegant; 聡富医雅 = a wise, rich and elegant female doctor; 奏婦偉雅 = a great elegant lady who plays music.

Attention-getting transcription: 鼠怖異阿 = a fearful strange African rat; 薮歩猪亜 = an Asian wild boar which walks around in the bush; 騒怖異蛙 = a noisy fearful strange frog.

Stacey

(m, f) Greek, "fruitful" (EGW)

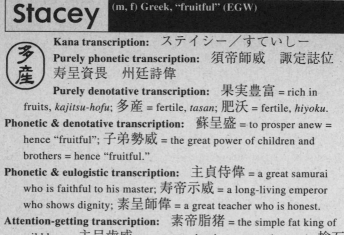

Kana transcription: ステイシー／すていしー

Purely phonetic transcription: 須帝師威　諏定誌位　寿呈資畏　州廷詩偉

Purely denotative transcription: 果実豊富 = rich in fruits, *kajitsu-hofu*; 多産 = fertile, *tasan*; 肥沃 = fertile, *hiyoku*.

Phonetic & denotative transcription: 蘇呈盛 = to prosper anew = hence "fruitful"; 子弟勢威 = the great power of children and brothers = hence "fruitful."

Phonetic & eulogistic transcription: 主貞侍偉 = a great samurai who is faithful to his master; 寿帝示威 = a long-living emperor who shows dignity; 素呈師偉 = a great teacher who is honest.

Attention-getting transcription: 素帝脂猪 = the simple fat king of wild boars; 主呈歯威 = a master who shows menacing teeth; 捨石井 = one who throws stones into the well.

Stanley

(m) Old English, "stony meadow" (ECS)

Kana transcription: スタンレイ／すたんれい

Purely phonetic transcription: 須堪令　諏丹励　寿担霊　州探玲　素耽嶺

Purely denotative transcription: 多石草地 = a stony meadow, *taseki-shochi*; 多石牧草地 = a stony meadow, *taseki-bokusochi*.

Phonetic & denotative transcription: 主嘆里懿 = a beautiful place of which the owner complains = hence a "stony meadow"; 素坦領 = a uncultivated flat territory = hence a "stony meadow."

Phonetic & eulogistic transcription: 主探麗 = a master who seeks elegance; 寿湛齢 = one who enjoys longevity; 司談麗 = an official who speaks elegantly; 姿端麗 = one who has a graceful appearance.

Attention-getting transcription: 主探霊 = a master who looks for a ghost; 司嘆齢 = an official who deplores his age.

Stephen
(m) Greek, "crown" (EGW)

Kana transcription: ステイーヴン／すていーぶん

Purely phonetic transcription: 須手位文　寿手偉聞
諏手畏分　素手威吻　捨移蚊　捨位紋

Purely denotative transcription: 冠 = a crown, *kanmuri*;
王冠 = a crown, *okan*; 花冠 = a crown, *kakan*; 英冠 = a crown,
eikan; 樹冠 = a crown, *jukan*.

Phonetic & denotative transcription: 守帝位豊運 = one which
defends the position of the emperor and brings good fortune = hence
a "crown"; 守帝位敷運 = a thing which brings and defends the
imperial position = hence a "crown."

Phonetic & eulogistic transcription: 素帝威問 = an honest emperor
who asks a dignified question; 司提偉文 = an official who submits
great documents.

Attention-getting transcription: 捨意吻 = one who has given up the
intention of kissing; 巣締蚊 = a mosquito which closes its nest.

Stewart
(m) Old English, "steward" (RGS)

Kana transcription: スチュワート／すちゅわーと

Purely phonetic transcription: 須中和亜徒
寿宙話雅途　諏注輪阿渡　州柱我跡

Purely denotative transcription: 家令 = a steward, *karei*;
執事 = a steward, *shitsuji*; 給仕長 = a steward, *kyujicho*; 司厨員
= a steward, *shichuin*.

Phonetic & denotative transcription: 主邸和雅努 = a chief who
tries to keep peace in the house = hence a "steward."

Phonetic & eulogistic transcription: 素智話雅頭 = an honest and
intelligent boss who talks elegantly; 司治和亜都 = an official who
rules an Asian city peacefully; 守知和雅頭 = a boss who defends a
wise and elegant peace.

Attention-getting transcription: 寿弟話唖頭 = a long-living elder
brother who talks about and laughs at his boss; 雛諦窪蛙土 = a
fledgling crying in a cave full of frogs.

Susannah

(f) Derived from "white lily" compounded with "grace" (HS)

Kana transcription: スザンナ／すざんな

Purely phonetic transcription: 須暫菜　寿残名　諏斬難　素残菜　州暫奈

Purely denotative transcription: 優雅白百合 = graceful white lily, *yuga-shirayuri*; 優美白倒仙 = graceful white lily, *yubi-hakutosan*; 上品白山慈姑 = graceful white lily, *johin-shiro-sanjiko*.

Phonetic & denotative transcription: 素残菜雅 = a graceful flower left blooming alone = hence a "graceful white lily."

Phonetic & eulogistic transcription: 寿残娜 = a beauty who remains long-living; 素残娜 = a beauty who remains honest; 主残名 = a master who left his name.

Attention-getting transcription: 雛残名 = a fledgling which remains famous; 蘇暫名 = one who resumes her fame temporarily; 洲残菜 = a flower left blooming in the sand bank.

Sylvia

(f) Latin, "wood" (EGW)

Kana transcription: シルヴィア／しるヴぃあ

Purely phonetic transcription: 師留美阿　誌瑠眉婀　詩漏琵雅　資琉備阿　試留避婀　知美亜

Purely denotative transcription: 木 = wood, *ki*; 木材 = wood, *mokuzai*; 材木 = wood, *mokuzai*; 森 = woods, *mori*; 林 = woods, *hayashi*; 森林 = woods, *shinrin*; 茂林 = woods, *morin*.

Phonetic & denotative transcription: 森留備雅 = a beautiful wood = "wood"; 枝留美雅 = branches which stay beautiful = a "wood."

Phonetic & eulogistic transcription: 姿留美雅 = one whose style stays beautiful and elegant; 至流魅婀 = a beauty who exudes charm; 姉留備雅 = an elder sister endowed with elegance.

Attention-getting transcription: 雌留微雅 = a slightly elegant woman; 姉留肥唖 = a fat elder sister who is laughing.

Tamara

(f) Russian, Hebrew, "palm tree" (RGS)

Kana transcription: タマラ／たまら

Purely phonetic transcription: 多真羅　田馬等
霊良　玉螺　珠等 or 手偉摩羅　廷間螺　帝摩等
貞真良　蹄馬螺　庭磨等

Purely denotative transcription: 椰子乃木 = a palm tree, *yashi-no-ki.*

Phonetic & denotative transcription: 多舞裸 = a branchless, or "naked," tree = hence a "palm tree."

Phonetic & eulogistic transcription: 大真良 = one who is extremely good; 妥磨良 = one who agrees to study goodness; 舵馬良 = one who guides a horse well = a good horse rider; 多真良 = one who has a lot of real good; 手偉真良 = one who has really great hands.

Attention-getting transcription: 惰真騾 = a really lazy mule; 田間螺 = a shell in the rice field; 大真蝸 = a large true snail.

Ted

(m) Pet form of Edward (LDWG); see Edward

Kana transcription: テッド／てっど

Purely phonetic transcription: 手度　弟努　廷奴
帝怒　偵度　禎努　低土

Purely denotative transcription:　See Edward

Phonetic & denotative transcription: 帝努 = a striving emperor = hence "rich"; 偵努 = to investigate vigilantly = hence "guardian."

Phonetic & eulogistic transcription: 呈努 = one who shows an effort; 貞童 = a faithful child; 弟能 = a capable younger brother; 鄭農 = a polite farmer.

Attention-getting transcription:　手努 = industrious hands; 帝怒 = an angry emperor; 抵奴 = a resistant fellow.

Terry

(m) Latin, "soft, tender" (ECS); pet form of Terence (LDWG)

Kana transcription: テリー／てりー

Purely phonetic transcription: 定礼　帝励　弟礼　禎麗　廷苓　定領　貞伶

Purely denotative transcription: 柔軟 = soft, *junan*; 柔和 = soft, *juwa*; 温和 = soft, *onwa*; 穏当 = soft, *onto*; 温厚 = soft, *onko* or 仁恕 = tender, *ninjo*; 親切 = tender, *shinsetsu*; 親愛 = tender, *shin-ai*.

Phonetic & denotative transcription: 呈礼 = to be courteous = hence "soft, tender."

Phonetic & eulogistic transcription: 禎礼 = one who is right and courteous; 帝令 = an imperial order; 弟礼 = a courteous brother; 帝怜 = a wise emperor; 帝礼 = a courteous emperor.

Attention-getting transcription: 帝冷 = a cold emperor; 醍霊 = a drunken ghost; 貞零 = one who has no chastity.

Theodore

(m) Greek, "God's gift" (EGW)

Kana transcription: セオドール／せおどーる

Purely phonetic transcription: 瀬緒動瑠　背尾童留　勢夫堂流　世雄同硫

Purely denotative transcription: 神乃進物 = a gift from God, *kami-no-shinmotsu*; 神乃贈品 = a gift from God, *kami-no-zohin*; 神乃恵物 = a gift from God, *kami-no-keibutsu*; 神乃贈遺 = a gift from God, *kami-no-zoi*.

Phonetic & denotative transcription: 施恵御努留 = divine efforts to provide benevolence = hence "god's gift."

Phonetic & eulogistic transcription: 正追努留 = one who tries to follow justice; 誠夫導留 = a sincere husband who guides his wife; 世王憧留 = the king the world adores.

Attention-getting transcription: 世雄度流 = a world-famous hero who was often exiled = hence "Napoleon"; 誓烏洞留 = a crow which makes an oath in a cave.

Theresa

(f) Greek, "the harvester" (ECS)

Kana transcription: テレサ／てれさ

Purely phonetic transcription: 手麗紗　手令唆
手嶺査　手励嵯　手鈴沙

Purely denotative transcription: 収穫者 = a harvester,
shukaku-sha; 刈取人 = a harvester, *karitorinin*; 刈入者 = a
harvester, *kariiresha*.

Phonetic & denotative transcription: 手励収 = hands which are
busy harvesting = hence a "harvester"; 手励作 = striving, working
hands = hence the hands of "the harvester."

Phonetic & eulogistic transcription: 呈麗作 = one who shows
elegant manners; 鄭礼差 = one who is outstanding in politeness and
courtesy; 禎麗査 = a chaste and elegant detective; 帝礼作 = one
who has royal manners.

Attention-getting transcription: 涕麗嵯 = a beauty who signs in
tears; 睇麗唆 = a beauty who winks suggestively; 手霊砂 = a
ghost's hand in the sand.

Thomas

(m) Aramic, "twin" (EGW)

Kana transcription: トーマス／とーます

Purely phonetic transcription: 棟間州　投魔素
燈馬諏　稲真守　登鱒　頭桝　刀益　統増

Purely denotative transcription: 二子 = a twin, *futago*; 双
子 = a twin, *futago*; 双生児 = a twin, *soseiji*; 双胎 = a twin, *sotai*.

Phonetic & denotative transcription: 等雄真双 = an equally heroic
real twin = hence a "twin."

Phonetic & eulogistic transcription: 闘真主 = a real fighting master;
頭真素 = a very honest boss; 徒磨素 = a person who practices
honesty; 闘真司 = a real fighting official.

Attention-getting transcription: 逃馬司 = an official who escapes on
a horse; 討魔首 = one who attacks a demon's neck.

Timothy
(m) Greek, compound of "time," "honor, respect" and "god" (EGW)

Kana transcription: テイモシー／ていもしー
Purely phonetic transcription: 手藻師位　手茂詩威
手裳試偉　手模資畏

Purely denotative transcription: 名誉神 = honor and god, *meiyo-shin*; 誉神 = honor and god, *homare-shin*; 栄誉神 = honor and god, *eiyo-kami*; 崇敬神 = honor and god, *sukei-kami*.

Phonetic & denotative transcription: 提最崇栄 = to provide the greatest respect and honor = hence "honor, respect."

Phonetic & eulogistic transcription: 提母資医 = one who sends a capable doctor to his mother; 弟模侍偉 = a younger brother who is a great model samurai; 帝猛姿威 = an emperor who shows a brave and dignified style; 鄭最司畏 = the most polite solemn official.

Attention-getting transcription: 帝摸師偉 = an emperor who imitates a great teacher; 抵猛司威 = one who shows fierce resistance to an arrogant official; 呈忙獅威 = a busy lion on the rampage.

Todd
(m) Surname, "fox-hunter," used as a first name (LDWG)

Kana transcription: トッド／とっど
Purely phonetic transcription: 途努　登度　徒怒
斗土　渡怒　都奴　杜土

Purely denotative transcription: 狐狩人 = a fox-hunter, *kitsune karyudo*; 狐猟師 = a fox-hunter, *kitsune yoshi*; 狐猟人 = a fox-hunter, *kitsune ryojin*; 狐猟者 = a fox-hunter, *kitsune ryosha*.

Phonetic & denotative transcription: 杜追度 = one who frequently chases (foxes) in the forest = hence a "fox-hunter"; 杜追努 = one who chases (foxes) in the forest = hence a "fox-hunter."

Phonetic & eulogistic transcription: 頭努 = a boss who makes an effort; 徒導 = one who guides students; 闘童 = a fighting child.

Attention-getting transcription: 妬度 = often jealous; 頭怒 = an angry boss; 兎吶 = a noisy rabbit; 賭奴 = a slave of gambling.

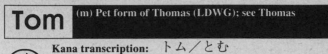

Tom (m) Pet form of Thomas (LDWG); see Thomas

瞳
務

Kana transcription: トム／とむ

Purely phonetic transcription: 都務　燈夢　稲舞
登霧　頭武　杜鵑　統武

Purely denotative transcription: See Thomas

Phonetic & denotative transcription: 瞳務 = the duty of (two) pupils = hence a "twin"; 瞳夢 = the dream of two pupils = hence a "twin."

Phonetic & eulogistic transcription: 頭武 = a samurai boss; 統務 = one who is in charge of the presidency = hence a president; 徒舞 = a dancing student; 闘武 = a fighting samurai.

Attention-getting transcription: 兎霧 = a rabbit in the fog; 都鵡 = a city parrot; 頭夢 = a dreaming boss.

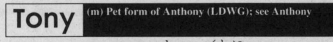

Tony (m) Pet form of Anthony (LDWG); see Anthony

討
児

Kana transcription: トニー／とにー

Purely phonetic transcription: 都荷　登児　途仁
徒丹　途爾　頭弐　杜仁

Purely denotative transcription: See Anthony

Phonetic & denotative transcription: 討児 = a man who attacks = hence "inestimable; strength"; 刀児 = a man with a sword = hence "inestimable; strength"; 狙児 = a man who plots an attack = "inestimable; strength."

Phonetic & eulogistic transcription: 頭児 = a child boss; 徒仁 = a benevolent man; 刀仁 = one who carries both a sword and benevolence; 都児 = a city child; 十仁 = one who does ten benevolent acts.

Attention-getting transcription: 逃児 = an child who escapes; 盗児 = a child who steals things; 十二 = a twelve-year old boy; 鼠丹 = a red mouse.

Tracy

(f) A diminutive of Theresa (EGW); see Theresa

Kana transcription: トレイシー／とれいしー

Purely phonetic transcription: 都礼司畏　頭励侍医 登齢司偉　渡怜師威

Purely denotative transcription: See Theresa

Phonetic & denotative transcription: 徒励収意 = a person who has an industrious intention to harvest = a "harvester."

Phonetic & eulogistic transcription: 渡戻詩偉 = a great wandering poet; 宕麗紫異 = an unusually elegant purple gem; 頭励至畏 = a solemnly industrious boss.

Attention-getting transcription: 杜礼脂猪 = a courteous fat wild boar in the forest; 逃怜獅偉 = a wise great lioness who runs away; 妬麗姉威 = a jealous, elegant and arrogant elder sister.

Brainteaser: 盆積飴 = a tray on which candies are placed; 盆海 = a wide and shallow sea. Note: "Tra-" (= tray) = 盆 and "-cy" (= sea) = 海 in Japanese. Hence both are read "Tracy."

Valerie

(f) Latin, "to be strong" (LDWG)

Kana transcription: ヴァレリ／ヴぁれり

Purely phonetic transcription: 芭令利　馬鈴璃 羽麗裏　場霊里　磨嶺離

Purely denotative transcription: 強壮 = to be strong, *kyoso*; 雄壮 = to be strong, *yuso*; 勇壮 = to be strong, *yuso*; 強豪 = to be strong, *kyogo*; 強大 = to be strong, *kyodai*; 強力 = to be strong, *kyoryoku*.

Phonetic & denotative transcription: 磨力礼 = to learn power and courtesy = hence "to be strong."

Phonetic & eulogistic transcription: 磨礼麗 = one who practices courtesy and elegance; 芭麗里 = one from a village of banana plants; 磨令吏 = an official who improves laws.

Attention-getting transcription: 馬礼利 = a courteous and clever horse; 罵霊離 = one who condemns a ghost in order to drive it away.

164

Veronica
(f) Latin, "true" & Greek, "figure, image, likeness"; meaning "ideal Saint" (HS)

Kana transcription: ヴェロニカ／べぇろにか

Purely phonetic transcription: 辺露爾華　部侶尼佳　琶炉丹家　辺呂仁賀　部魯荷貨　琶路弐香

Purely denotative transcription: 理想聖人 = an ideal Saint, *riso-seijin* or 基督乃真像 = the true image of Christ, *kirisuto-shinzo*; 基督実像 = the true image of Christ, *kirisuto-jitsuzo*; 基督真正像 = the true image of Christ, *kirisuto-shoshinzo*.

Phonetic & denotative transcription: 美露似画 = a portrait = "figure, image, or likeness."

Phonetic & eulogistic transcription: 辺露仁嫁 = a benevolent bride surrounded by dew drops; 部朗尼華 = a cheerful and brilliant nun in the village; 琶侶尼誇 = a proud nun who is accompanied by a Japanese mandolin.

Attention-getting transcription: 部驢荷嫁 = a village donkey which carries a bride; 辺露丹鹿 = a red deer which appears around here.

Victor
(m) Latin, "conqueror" (EGW)

Kana transcription: ヴィクター／びくたー

Purely phonetic transcription: 美究多亜　魅久太阿　眉玖茶雅　備功舵亜

Purely denotative transcription: 征服者 = a conqueror, *seifukusha*; 勝利者 = a conqueror, *shorisha*.

Phonetic & denotative transcription: 避駆他 = one who now drives out the other (people) = hence, a "conqueror"; 備苦他 = one who causes others pain = hence a "conqueror."

Phonetic & eulogistic transcription: 魅公多雅 = a charming duke who is full of elegance; 備功大雅 = one who has many excellent merits; 備駒多亜 = one who has many Asian horses; 毘苦救他 = one who helps and saves others in trouble.

Attention-getting transcription: 肥狗惰亜 = a lazy, fat Asian dog; 鼻紅蛇阿 = an African snake with a red nose.

Victoria  (f) Feminine form of Victor (HS); see Victor

Kana transcription: ヴィクトリア／びくとりあ

Purely phonetic transcription: 美究多利婀
魅久都理阿　眉玖頭麗雅　備功途吏唖

Purely denotative transcription: See Victor

Phonetic & denotative transcription: 避駆倒離婀 = a
beauty who now drives (people) away and beats them down =
hence, a "female conqueror"; 備苦逃離婀 = a beauty who causes
(others) pain and lets them run away = a "female conqueror."

Phonetic & eulogistic transcription: 美究多利婀 = a clever beauty
who seeks a lot of beauty; 魅久頭理阿 = an eternally charming
and wise African boss; 眉玖徒麗雅 = a beautiful and elegant
person who has gem-like eyes; 備功多吏婀 = a beautiful female
official who has lots of merits.

Attention-getting transcription: 肥狗杜離阿 = a fat African dog
leaving the forest; 鼻紅兎麗亜 = an elegant African rabbit with a
pink nose; 美駒多利唖 = a beautiful and clever laughing horse.

Vincent (m) Latin, "conquering" (EGW)

Kana transcription: ヴィンセント／びんせんと

Purely phonetic transcription: 頻船渡　便先途
瓶栓頭　便踐都　頻戰渡

Purely denotative transcription: 征服 = conquering,
seifuku; 勝利 = conquering, *shori*; 克服 = conquering, *kokufuku*.

Phonetic & denotative transcription: 敏戰頭 = a swiftly fighting
chief = "conquering"; 頻戰倒 = frequently fighting and beating =
"conquering"; 敏戰闘 = to fight swiftly = "conquering."

Phonetic & eulogistic transcription: 敏戰徒 = a swiftly fighting
person; 頻占頭 = a boss who constantly interferes; 便船頭 = a
boss of a cargo ship; 頻戰闘 = one who fights frequently.

Attention-getting transcription: 貧賤徒 = a poor wretched person;
頻羨頭 = a very jealous boss; 敏遷党 = a political party whose
platform changes frequently.

166

Virginia

(f) Latin, "spring"; "flourishing" (HS); often mistakenly associated with "virgin"

Kana transcription: ヴァージニア／ばーじにあ

Purely phonetic transcription: 芭亜慈仁亜
羽雅茨荷雅　場阿滋丹阿　磨亜磁尼亜

Purely denotative transcription: 処女 = a virgin, *shojo*; 季女 = a virgin, *kijo*; 生娘 = a virgin, *kimusume* or 繁栄 = flourishing, *hanei*; 繁盛 = flourishing, *hanjo*.

Phonetic & denotative transcription: 磨雅除妊婀 = a beauty who practices elegance, but avoids pregnancy = hence a "virgin."

Phonetic & eulogistic transcription: 磨慈尼雅 = an elegant nun who practices benevolence; 馬持尼雅 = an elegant nun who owns a horse; 芭雅持仁婀 = a benevolent beauty with a beautiful flower.

Attention-getting transcription: 罵蛙寺尼雅 = an elegant nun who condemns a frog in the temple; 婆飼弐鴉 = an old woman who keeps two crows.

Walter

(m) Germanic, compound of "rule" and "folk, people" (RGS)

Kana transcription: ウオルター／うおるたー

Purely phonetic transcription: 宇王留太阿
右応硫田亜　雨欧瑠多雅　迂往流汰亜

Purely denotative transcription: 治民 = rule and folk, *chimin*; 支配国民 = rule and folk, *shihai-kokumin*; 統治民族 = rule and folk, *tochi-minzoku*.

Phonetic & denotative transcription: 宇王留統雅 = the heavenly king stays to rule in an elegant manner = hence "rule."

Phonetic & eulogistic transcription: 優夫流茶 = a kind husband who prepares tea; 優雄留他 = a kind hero who accommodates others; 有王瑠大雅 = a king who has large elegant gems; 右王留多 = one who helps the king very much.

Attention-getting transcription: 鵜小留田雅 = a small cormorant which stays in a fine rice field; 烏雄留田唖 = a crow which is laughing in the rice field.

William
(m) Germanic, compound of "will" and "helmet" (RGS)

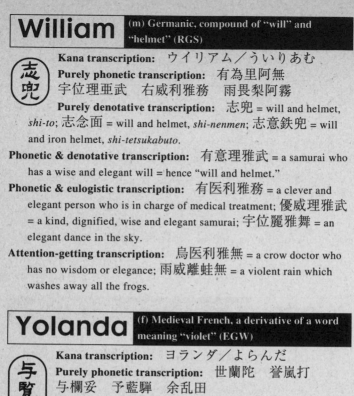

Kana transcription: ウイリアム／ういりあむ

Purely phonetic transcription: 有為里阿無
宇位理亜武　右威利雅務　雨畏梨阿霧

Purely denotative transcription: 志兜 = will and helmet, *shi-to*; 志念面 = will and helmet, *shi-nenmen*; 志意鉄兜 = will and iron helmet, *shi-tetsukabuto*.

Phonetic & denotative transcription: 有意理雅武 = a samurai who has a wise and elegant will = hence "will and helmet."

Phonetic & eulogistic transcription: 有医利雅務 = a clever and elegant person who is in charge of medical treatment; 優威理雅武 = a kind, dignified, wise and elegant samurai; 宇位麗雅舞 = an elegant dance in the sky.

Attention-getting transcription: 烏医利雅無 = a crow doctor who has no wisdom or elegance; 雨威離蛙無 = a violent rain which washes away all the frogs.

Yolanda
(f) Medieval French, a derivative of a word meaning "violet" (EGW)

Kana transcription: ヨランダ／よらんだ

Purely phonetic transcription: 世蘭陀　誉嵐打
与欄妥　予藍驒　余乱田

Purely denotative transcription: 菫 = violet, *sumire*; 金草 = violet, *kinso*; 笈菫 = violet, *kyukin*; 鳥啄 = violet, *chotaku*.

Phonetic & denotative transcription: 与覧唾 = mouth-wateringly beautiful = "violet"; 世覧打 = one who seems to strike out at the world in rage = "violet."

Phonetic & eulogistic transcription: 世覧娜 = a beauty who sees the world; 耀蘭大 = a large shining orchid; 誉乱打 = one who plans an honorable uprising; 与良運舵 = one who is given good luck and guidance.

Attention-getting transcription: 世乱蛇 = a boa which panics the world; 夜嵐打 = a storm which hits at night; 与乱蛇 = a snake which causes a panic.

Kanji
for
Last Names
(and additional first names)

Last Names (and additional first names)

Perhaps by now, you have selected an exciting kanji combination for your personal name, but wish you could transcribe your surname, as well. Or maybe you have a rare or exotic personal name that the first part of this book failed to cover. This section of the book is for people who wish to render their family names into Japanese, and also for those people whose first names did not appear in the first section of the book.

The sounds in the table beginning on page 175 are phonetic building blocks which you can put together to create an appropriate kanji combination for either of your names. The fact that there are some important but simple differences between the phonetic systems of English and Japanese, though, means it is necessary to understand a few basic rules about Japanese sounds before getting started.

Although there is a great deal of phonetic overlap between the two languages, there are some big differences, as well. In particular, Japanese lacks a number of the sounds used in English and compensates by approximating them with Japanese sounds. The following Japanese sounds are generally used to approximate their English counterparts:

a   approximates "u," as in "bug."

aa   approximates "r" after a vowel, unless another vowel follows the "r."

au   approximates "ow," as in "power."

b   approximates "v."

h   approximates "f."

oa   approximates "aw," as in "awe."

r   approximates "r" before a vowel.

ru   appoximates "l" before a consonant, or at the end of a syllable.

s   approximates "th."

shi	approximates	"si," as in "sin" and "she," as in "sheet."
tsu	approximates	"too,"as in "tooth."
u	approximates	"w."
z	approximates	"th," as in "they."

It is also important to keep in mind that Japanese phonetics are not based on "simple" sounds, but on whole syllables. Therefore, the language does not have the independent consonant sounds that often end English-language syllables, like the "s" sound at the end of Thomas, or "k" sound that ends the first syllable of Jackson. Rather, for each consonant stem, Japanese has five vowel combinations: Thus, instead of having just m, we have the syllables ma, mi, mu, me, and mo. Where possible, Japanese avoids having to approximate the independent consonants of English by connecting the consonants to the vowels that follow them, in names like Kelly, David, and Daniel. Where this is impossible because there are no following vowels, however, as in the cases of Thomas and Jackson above, Japanese does its best to approximate independent consonant sounds.

English independent consonants are generally approximated through use of the appropriate Japanese consonant with *u, i,* or *o* tacked on. "Simple" English consonants are transcribed into Japanese as follows:

"b" becomes	*bu*
"d" becomes	*do*
"ch"becomes	*chi*
"f" becomes	*fu*
"g" becomes	*gu*
"h" becomes	*fu*
"j" becomes	*ji*
"k" becomes	*ku*
"l" becomes	*ru*

"m" becomes	*mu*
"p" becomes	*pu*
"r" becomes	*ru*
"s" becomes	*su*
"sh" becomes	*shi*
"t" becomes	*to*
"ts" becomes	*tsu*
"v" becomes	*bu*
"z" becomes	*zu*

The exception to this rule is the English "n" sound. In Japanese, there is an independent n, but it appears only as the final sound in a syllable—never at the beginning. There are, therefore, no kanji that have just an n sound (n can only be written with kana). This book addresses that problem by providing kanji for syllables ending in n: for instance, kan, kin, ken, kun, and kon.

Let's look at a few examples and see where all this gets us:

Bob	becomes	*Bobu*
Clark	becomes	*Kuraaku*
Herbert	becomes	*Haabaato*
Jackson	becomes	*Jakuson*
Jones	becomes	*Jonzu*
Leslie	becomes	*Resurii*
Munson	becomes	*Manson*
Smith	becomes	*Sumisu*
Theodore	becomes	*Shiodoaa*
Thomas	becomes	*Tomasu*
Thompson	becomes	*Tomupuson*
Washington	becomes	*Washiinguton*
William	becomes	*Uiruyamu*

Once you've worked out the Japanization of your name, selecting the kanji for it is easy. For instance, for Bob, you'd simply select a kanji for bo and one for bu. For Munson, you'd pick kanji for mu, un, and son. For Herbert, you would use the characters for ha, a, ba, a, and to.

By following these simple rules, you, too, should be able to write your own name in kanji easily, whether your name be Elijah Muhammed, or Siobhan O'Connell.

Phonetic transcription table

a あ ア	亜	Asia	an あん アン	安	peace
	阿	Africa		案	plan
	雅	elegant		杏	apricot
	婀	beauty		諳	to memorize
	唖	to laugh		鞍	saddle
i い イ	伊偉	Italy	in いん イン	員	member
	偉	great		院	ex-emperor
	意	intention		引	to pull
	医	doctor		印	stamp
	委	committee		韻	rhyme
u う ウ	雨	rain	un うん ウン	運	luck
	宇	cosmos		雲	cloud
	憂	cormorant		暈	halo
	右	right (side)		慍	angry
	優	excellent			
e え エ	恵	benevolent	en えん エン	円	circle
	江	inlet		園	garden
	衛	guard		宴	banquet
	慧	wisdom		演	performance
	絵	drawing		塩	salt
o お オ	緒	string	on おん オン	恩	indebtedness
	夫	husband		温	warm
	雄	hero		音	sound
	尾	tail		穏	mild
	御	honorific		御	honorific

ka かカ	華	floweriness	kan かんカン	勘	intuition
	嘉	auspicious		官	official
	歌	song		感	feeling
	香	smell		幹	trunk
	加	to add		冠	crown
ki きキ	貴	noble	kin きんキン	金	gold
	喜	glad		勤	work
	紀	period		欽	emperor
	規	rule		謹	respectful
	希	rare		欣	glad
ku くク	句	phrase	kun くんクン	君	lord
	久	eternal		勲	merit
	倶	club		訓	lesson
	究	to master		薫	fragrance
	苦	pain		輝	chaps
ke けケ	家	house	ken けんケン	剣	sword
	毛	hair		検	inspection
	化	ghost		権	right
	佳	fair		健	healthy
	花	flower		賢	wise
ko こコ	鼓	hand-drum	kon こんコン	混	to mix
	狐	fox		根	root
	固	solid		紺	blue
	庫	storage		魂	spirit
	誇	pride		婚	to marry

sa さ サ	早 査 沙 瑳 唆	early search sand to polish to urge	**san** さん サン	参 算 産 燦 賛	to join to calculate to produce bright to praise
shi し シ	市 史 師 志 詩	market history teacher intention poem	**shin** しん シン	新 慎 信 真 神	new prudent to believe true god
su す ス	洲 諏 須 寿 巣	sand bank to consult necessary longevity nest	**sun** すん スン	寸 洲暈 諏運 寿雲	inch sand bank, halo consult, fortune longevity, cloud
se せ セ	世 施 背 瀬 畝	world alms back rapid 1/4 acre	**sen** せん セン	戦 千 仙 線 泉	fight thousand hermit line fountain
so そ ソ	祖 礎 僧 素 蘇	ancestor basis increase white to revive	**son** そん ソン	尊 存 村 損 遜	to respect to exist village loss humility

ta た タ	多	many	tan たん タン	担	to shoulder
	田	rice field		単	single
	太	first		探	to search
	他	other		鍛	to train
	汰	to select		端	neat
chi ち チ	知	knowledge	chin ちん チン	朕	emperor
	置	to put		鎮	to calm down
	値	value		珍	rare
	治	to rule		椿	camellia
	地	earth		沈	to sink
tsu つ ツ	津	harbor	tsun つん ツン	津運	harbor, fortune
	通	to pass		通薀	to pass, angry
	都	capital		都雲	capital, cloud
te て テ	手	hand	ten てん テン	天	heaven
				展	to extend
				点	point
				転	to roll
				店	shop
to と ト	頭	head	ton とん トン	問	to ask
	徒	disciple		頓	to stay
	都	capital city		豚	pig
	斗	to measure		屯	to gather
	図	chart		敦	sincere

na な な	名 菜 南 那 娜	name vegetable south peaceful beautiful	**nan** なん ナン	南 男 楠 軟 難	south man camphor tree soft hard
ni に ニ	荷 弐 尼 丹 煮	charge two nun red to boil	**nin** にん ニン	人 任 忍 認 仁	man duty to endure to accept considerate
nu ぬ ヌ	怒 奴	angry chap	**nun** ぬん ヌン	怒雲 奴蘊	angry, cloud chap, angry
ne ね ネ	根 値 音 鼠 嶺	root value sound rat summit	**nen** ねん ネン	年 念 粘 捻 撚	year to concentrate sticky to twist to burn
no の ノ	野 乃 之	field namely of	**non** のん ノン	暖 呑 暢	warm to drink to grow

ha/fa は ハ ふぁ ファ	覇	leader	han はん ハン	帆	sail
	派	group		判	to judge
	波	wave		反	reverse
	葉	leaf		版	edition
	破	to break		範	model
hi/fi ひ ヒ ふぃ フィ	秘	secret	hin ひん ヒン	賓	guest
	妃	princess		品	article
	比	to compare		貧	poor
	飛	to fly		頻	frequent
	日	sun		浜	beach
hu/fu ふ フ	父	father	fun ふん フン	分	to divide
	婦	woman		奮	to endeavor
	布	cloth		憤	angry
	賦	to provide		吻	lip
	譜	notation		噴	to spurt
he/fe へ ヘ ふぇ フェ	戸	door	hen へん ヘン	辺	region
	屁	flatulence		変	to change
				篇	volume
				返	to return
				片	piece
ho/fo ほ ホ ふぉ フォ	帆	sail	hon ほん ホン	本	book
	穂	ear		奔	to run
	歩	step		反	to oppose
	補	assistant		翻	to translate
	保	to keep		笨	poor

ma ま マ	馬 horse 磨 to polish 真 true 摩 abrasion 魔 devil	man まん マン	満 full 万 ten thousand 慢 lazy 懣 angry 鰻 eel
mi み ミ	魅 charm 美 beautiful 実 fruit 味 taste 眉 eyebrow	min みん ミン	民 people 明 bright 眠 to sleep 憫 to pity 罠 snare
mu む ム	務 charge 武 samurai 舞 dance 夢 dream 霧 fog	mun むん ムン	務薀 charge, to pile 武運 martial, fortune 霧雲 fog, cloud 舞暈 dance, halo 夢薀 dream, disorder
me め メ	目 eye 雌 female 女 woman 瑪 jade 芽 sprout	men めん メン	面 face 免 to evade 綿 cotton 麺 noodle 湎 to sink
mo も モ	模 model 茂 rank 裳 clothes 藻 weed 母 mother	mon もん モン	紋 emblem 門 gate 文 sentence 問 to ask 聞 to hear

ya や ヤ	夜 night 耶 father 矢 arrow 野 field 屋 house	yan やん ヤン	矢暗 arrow, dark 野案 field, suggestion 屋杏 house, apricot 夜安 night, peace
yu ゆ ユ	由 reason 諭 to lead 愉 pleasant 輸 to carry 癒 to cure	yun ゆん ユン	諭雲 to lead, cloud 愉運 pleasant, fortune 輸暈 to carry, halo 由薀 reason, to pile 癒温 to cure, warm
yo よ ヨ	世 world 代 age 誉 honor 豫 to forecast 与 to give	yon よん ヨン	四 four 代暈 age, halo 誉雲 honor, cloud 世運 world, fortune
ra/la ら ラ	良 good 鑼 gong 蘿 ivy 等 companion 羅 silk	ran/lan らん ラン	蘭 orchid 藍 basket 覧 to look 嵐 storm 乱 disorder
ri/li り リ	理 reason 利 profit 吏 official 里 village 俐 clever	rin/lin りん リン	林 forest 輪 circle 倫 ethical 鈴 bell 隣 next

ru/lu			run/lun		
る	瑠	gem	るん	瑠雲	gem, cloud
レ	留	to stay	ルン	留運	to stay, fortune
	流	to flow		流暈	to flow, halo
	屢	frequent		琉薀	gem, to pile
	琉	gem			

re/le			ren/len		
れ	麗	beautiful	れん	連	to connect
レ	礼	courteous	レン	練	to train
	霊	spirit		恋	love
	嶺	summit		簾	curtain
	怜	wise		廉	cheap

ro/lo			ron/lon		
ろ	露	dew	ろん	論	theory
ロ	慮	considerate	ロン	崙	steep
	侶	companion		乱	disorder
	路	road			
	炉	furnace			

wa			wan		
わ	和	accord	わん	湾	bay
ワ	環	circle	ワン	腕	arm
	琶	lute		椀	bowl
	儘	Japan			

ga が ガ	牙 雅 賀 鵞 芽	tusk elegant felicitation goose sprout	**gan** がん ガン	岩 巌 願 顔 岸	rock severe wish face shore
gi ぎ ギ	義 技	morals technique	**gin** ぎん ギン	銀 吟	silver recital
gu ぐ グ	紅 求 遇	red to search to meet	**gun** ぐん グン	郡 群 軍	county group army
ge げ ゲ	牙 夏 華	tusk summer flower	**gen** げん ゲン	厳 限 現 元	severe limit present root
go ご ゴ	護 御 后	to defend honorific empress	**gon** ごん ゴン	言 権 欣 金	to say right glad gold

za ざ ザ	座 坐 挫	seat to sit to collapse	zan ざん ザン	暫 残 斬 塹 慙	provisional remains to cut, to kill moat shame
zi/ji じ ジ	字 慈 児 治 示	letter benevolent child to cure to show	zin/jin じん ジン	人 神 仁 塵 迅	man god charity dust rapid
zu ず ヅ	頭 図 逗 豆 杜	head figure to stay bean forest	zun ずん ズン	図員 頭運	diagram, member head, fate
ze ぜ ゼ	是 税 誓	right tax vow	zen ぜん ゼン	全 善 禅 繕 然	all virtue zen to repair yes
zo ぞ ゾ	曽 像 蔵 造 増	to pile image storage to make increase	zon ぞん ゾン	存 増運 造雲	to exist increase, fate to make, clouds

da だ ダ	打 hit 陀 Buddha 兌 exchange 妥 peaceful 舵 rudder	dan だん ダン	団 group 談 talk 段 step
di ぢ ヂ	see "ji"	din じん ジン	see "jin"
du づ ヅ	see "zu"	dun づん ヅン	see "zun"
de で デ	弟 younger brother 出 coming out 袮	den でん デン	澱 to sink 田 rice field 殿 building 電 electric
do ど ド	度 angry 努 effort	don どん ドン	鈍 dull 丼 bowl 曇 cloudy

ba/va ば バ ばぁ ヴァ	婆 芭 罵	old woman plantain to condemn	**ban** ばん バン	番 盤 晩 蛮 伴	turn table evening savage to accompany
bi/vi び ビ びぃ ヴィ	備 媚 美	to equip coquette pretty	**bin** びん ビン	便 敏 瓶 頻 貧	convenient swift bottle frequent poor
bu/vu ぶ ブ ヴ	武 舞 負 豊 部	samurai dance to lose rich department	**bun** ぶん ブン	文 聞 分 紋	sentence to hear to divide emblem
be/ve べ ベ べぇ ヴェ	部 辺	department region	**ben** べん ベン	弁 勉 鞭	valve to study whip
bo/vo ぼ ボ ぼぉ ヴォ	母 慕 募 模	mother to adore to collect model	**bon** ぼん ボン	盆 梵 凡 煩	plate sacred ordinary trouble

pa ぱ パ	葉 破 羽	leaf to break feather	pan ぱん パン	版 班 判 犯 般	edition group to judge crime to circulate
pi ぴ ピ	費 泌 日	expense secretion sun	pin ぴん ピン	品 日引 飛引	article day, pull fly, pull
pu ぷ プ	符 婦 豊	notation woman rich	pun ぷん プン	分 吻 奮	minute lip to endeavor
pe ぺ ペ	兵 併 平 餅	soldier to merge flat rice cake	pen ぺん ペン	片 辺 編 変	piece region volume change
po ぽ ポ	葡 舗 保	wine shop to keep	pon ぽん ポン	本 帆	book sail

kya きゃ キャ	輝夜 bright, night 貴矢 noble, arrow	kyan きゃん キャン	喜安 glad, peace 貴鞍 noble, saddle
kyu きゅ キュ	急 urgent 求 to seek 救 to save	kyun きゅん キュン	急雲 urgent, cloud 球運 globe, fortune
kyo きょ キョ	居 domicile 挙 to raise 巨 giant 拠 to refuse 許 to permit	kyon きょん キョン	居音 domicile, sound 許恩 to permit, debt 挙温 to raise, warm
sha しゃ シャ	謝 to thank 偺 luxury 社 shrine 射 shooting 赦	shan しゃん シャン	社案 shrine, suggestion 射鞍 to shoot, saddle 写杏 describe, apricot
shu しゅ シュ	主 master 首 head 珠 pearl	shun しゅん シュン	峻 steep 春 spring 瞬 moment 俊 intelligent

sho しょ ショ	諸 various 曙 aurora 初 first 所 place	shon しょん ション	初恩 first, debt 署怨 police, grudge 諸音 various, sound
cha ちゃ チャ	茶 tea 茗 drank	chan ちゃん チャン	茶餡 tea, bean paste 茗安 drank, safe
chu ちゅ チュ	注 to pour 宙 cosmos 柱 pillar 忠 loyalty 註 to order	chun ちゅん チュン	注雲 to pour, cloud 宙運 cosmos, fortune
cho ちょ チョ	著 work 貯 to save	chon ちょん チョン	著音 work, sound 貯恩 to save, debt
nya にゃ ニャ	仁雅 kind, elegant 尼婀 nun, helper	nyan にゃん ニャン	仁安 kind, peaceful 尼諳 nun, memorize

190

nyu にゅ ニュ	入 to enter 乳 milk 柔 soft	nyun にゅん ニュン	乳雲 milk, cloud 入運 to enter, fortune
nyo にょ ニョ	女 woman 如 exactly	nyon にょん ニョン	女恩 woman, debt 仁穏 kind, calm
hya ひゃ ヒャ	冷 cool 飛矢 to fly, arrow 秘夜 secret, night	hyan ひゃん ヒャン	飛安 to fly, safe 秘案 secret, incident
hyu ひゅ ヒュ	日優 day, excellent 妃友 princess, friend 秘勇 secret, brave 飛右 to fly, right 灯夕 lamp, evening	hyun ひゅん ヒュン	秘勇運 secret, brave, fate 飛優雲 fly, superb, cloud
hyo ひょ ヒョ	票 vote 表 chart 評 comment 氷 ice	hyon ひょん ヒョン	評音 comment, sound 票恩 vote, debt 表温 surface, warm

mya みゃ ミャ	宮　palace 御屋　honorific, house 魅野　charm, field 美矢　beautiful, arrow 眉夜　eyebrow, night	**myan** みゃん ミャン	味餡　taste, bean paste 魅案　charm, suggestion 美杏　nut, apricot
myu みゅ ミュ	魅湯　charm, hot water 実油　nut, oil	**myun** みゅん ミュン	美愉雲　beautiful, fun 　　　cloud 魅裕員　charming, 　　　pretty, member
myo みょ ミョ	明　bright 妙　excellent 名　name	**myon** みょん ミョン	妙雲　excellent, cloud 明運　bright, fate
rya りゃ リャ	麗唖 利婀　profit, beauty 俐雅　clever, elegant	**ryan** りゃん リャン	理諳　reason, memorize 利安　profit, peace 悧案　clever, suggestion
ryu りゅ リュ	流　to flow 隆　prosperous 竜　dragon 留　to stay	**ryun** りゅん リュン	隆運　prosperous, fate 竜雲　dragon, cloud

ryo りょ リョ	領 rule 良 good 涼 cool	**ryon** りょん リョン	良穏 good, calm 涼飲 cool, drink
gya ぎゃ ギャ	義雅 justice, elegant 妓婀 geisha, beauty	**gyan** ぎゃん ギャン	議案 consult, suggest 技諳 skill, memorize
gyu ぎゅ ギュ	牛 cow	**gyun** ぎゅん ギュン	牛雲 cow, cloud 牛運 cow, fate
gyo ぎょ ギョ	行 go 仰 look upward 暁 dawn	**gyon** ぎょん ギョン	凝音 frozen, sound 行温 go, heat
ja じゃ ジャ	社 shrine 邪 evil 蛇 serpent 闍 tower 麝 musk	**jan** じゃん ジャン	治安 politics, peace 慈案 kind, plan

193

ju じゅ ジュ	受 to receive 寿 longevity	jun じゅん ジュン	順 order 純 pure 淳 sincere
jo じょ ジョ	序 order 助 help 女 woman	jon じょん ジョン	時音 time, sound 示温 show, warmth
bya びゃ ビャ	備矢 to equip, arrow 媚夜 coquette, night 美野 beautiful, field	byan びゃん ビャン	備矢運 to equip, arrow, fate 媚夜暈 coquette, night, halo
byu びゅ ビュ	魅優 charming, kind 美勇 beautiful, brave	byun びゅん ビュン	魅遊雲 charm, play, cloud 美優暈 beautiful, kind, halo
byo びょ ビョ	秒 second 描 to describe 鋲 rivet 錨 anchor 苗 seedling	byon びょん ビョン	秒運 second, fate 描員 draw, member

pya ぴゃ ピャ	費屋 expense, house 泌夜 secretion, night 日谷 sun, valley	pyan ぴゃん ピャン	費屋運 expense, house, fate 日谷暈 sun, valley, halo
pyu ぴゅ ピュ	併油 to merger, oil 蔽由 to cover, reason 兵愉 soldier, pleasant	pyun ぴゅん ピュン	併油雲 to merger, oil, cloud 平湯運 normal, hot water, luck
pyo ぴょ ピョ	表 chart 票 vote 俵 straw-bag 評 criticism 氷 ice	pyon ぴょん ピョん	表云 chart, to say 票運 vote, luck 俵雲 straw-bag, cloud 氷暈 ice, halo

Bibliography

Note: The abbreviations which follow each entry in parentheses correlate used to denote sources for each meaning provided for the English first names in the first part of the book.

Dunkling, Leslie Alan. *The Guinness Book of Names*. Middlesex: Guinness Publishing, 1995. (LD)

Dunkling, Leslie, and Gosling, William. *The Dictionary of First Names*. Melbourne: J.M. Dent and Sons, 1987. (LDWG)

World Book, Inc. *The World Book Dictionary*. New York: World Book, Inc., 1970. (ECS)

Kenkyusha, Ltd. *Kenkyusha's New English-Japanese Dictionary*. Tokyo: Kenkyusha, Ltd., 1980. (KID)

Shogakukan, Inc. *Shogakukan Random House English-Japanese Dictionary*. Tokyo: Shogakukan, Inc., 1973.

The World Publishing Company. *Webster's New World Dictionary of the American Language*. Cleveland: The World Publishing Company, 1959. (WNWD)

Stewart, George R. *American Given Names*. Translated by Y. Kimura. Tokyo: The Hokuseido Press, 1983. (GRS)

Swan, Helena. *Girls' Christian Names*. Rutland, Vermont: Charles E. Tuttle Publishing, 1973. (HS)

Withycombe, E.G. *The Oxford Dictionary of English Christian Names*. New York: Oxford University Press, 1977. (EGW)